SPIRIT
RECOVERY
MEDICINE BAG

SPIRIT
RECOVERY
MEDICINE BAG

A Transformational Guidebook for Living Happy, Joyous, and Free

Lee McCormick and Mary Faulkner

Health Communications, Inc.
Deerfield Beach, Florida

www.hcibooks.com

**Library of Congress Cataloging-in-Publication Data
is available through the Library of Congress**

© 2014 Lee McCormick and Mary Faulkner

ISBN-13: 978-0-7573-1794-1 (Paperback)
ISBN-10: 0-7573-1794-4 (Paperback)
ISBN-13: 978-0-7573-1794-4 (ePub)
ISBN-10: 0-7573--1795-2 (ePub)

Publisher: Health Communications, Inc.
        3201 S.W. 15th Street
        Deerfield Beach, FL 33442–8190

Cover image ©Heather Muro
Cover design by Dane Wesolko
Interior design by Lawna Patterson Oldfield
Interior formatting by Dawn Von Strolley Grove

Contents

Introduction

I f you have more than a few self-help books on your nightstand, why would you want to add *Spirit Recovery Medicine Bag* to the stack? One reason might have to do with the nature of self-help books. Many of these books have some good ideas, and they work sometimes for some people, at least for a while. Perhaps you got a temporary fix—scratched the itch—but if you are still searching, you probably did not experience the healing you seek. *Spirit Recovery Medicine Bag* isn't about fixing or scratching; it's about healing and growing.

Many self-help books, as well as most traditional therapies, operate from a compartmentalized mind-set. They isolate symptoms and treat them as being independent of one another—managing, micromanaging, and often overmedicating. They fail to look at a person as a whole human system in relationship with self, in relationship with others, and in relationship with the natural world. Compartmentalized strategies are focused on the problem and are organized around illness. They can be fine for a time for those seeking immediate help, but when the strategies fail to focus on letting go of the illness and old beliefs to make room for expansion and personal truth, their usefulness becomes debatable.

Spirit Recovery Medicine Bag is organized around wellness; it honors the life within you. The varied practices in this book connect you to your inborn desire for wholeness and your amazing ability to find it when you give yourself the right instructions and get out of your own way. Your desire to heal—to feel whole—is probably why you were willing to buy one more book and try one more time. That desire is your life insisting on being lived.

Put this book down for a moment and close your eyes. Take a few deep breaths until you feel yourself settling in. Ask yourself the following three questions:

- What do I want or what am I seeking?
- How will I feel when I get it?
- Where in my body do I feel it?

Once you have answered these three questions, pause and sit with your feelings. Your answers may change down the road, but, for now, accept the answers that come to you. Then, after a few moments, ask yourself the next question, but don't attempt to answer it.

- What needs to transform within me for me to experience the healing and growth I seek?

Hold the question. In other words, simply sit with it in your consciousness without trying to come up with answers. When you move too fast, you rush to fill your own void, and what you end up filling it with may not even skim the surface. This time you're going for something deeper and bigger. It may take a few weeks or even longer to get your internal system hooked up to really be able to answer this question. During this holding period, your internal search engine will be gathering insight. Healing comes as you learn to be comfortable holding the space while an older and wiser part of you begins to build a new neural network that will take you where you want to go—on a journey toward wholeness.

Spirit Recovery Medicine Bag launches you on this journey. Part One contains Lee's story of transformation, which he wrote ten years ago. His story sheds light on his early recovery process and how his concept of personal growth expanded beyond the traditional models. Exploring recovery from another's point of view is helpful for discovering what resonates with you and what you might like to try for yourself. Lee's story introduces you to some of the practices discussed in the second half of the book.

Part Two offers suggestions for your medicine bag. A medicine bag traditionally holds within it sacred objects that bring about healing, and, while the information and practices we're offering may not be "sacred" according to mainstream understanding, their transformative power is magical when they are approached with honesty and a true desire to change and grow. These practices aren't new. They take you into the ancient world of the artist and the shaman where you can tap into the innate creativity of imagination—of *dreaming*. What's probably new to you is the concept of *dreaming* your healing. As you learn to use your imagination in this way, you change your basic assumption from sick and dependent to healthy and free. You give your mind permission to do what it does best: to make something new for you.

We call this power of imagination the Inner Healer in recognition of its instinctive nature. It's already within you, and your Inner Healer knows what you need and how to find it. Your Inner Healer isn't limited by the constrictions of time and place. It is nonlinear—living the past, present, and future all at once. Your Inner Healer moves freely through time and space, healing the past and focusing you in the present where you can create your future with clear vision—rather than yet another rerun of your history.

On the Road of Happy Destiny

Spirit Recovery is for people who desire more out of life and are willing to put more of themselves into it and live more fully. It is for people who are willing to say yes to life—and sink their teeth into that commitment. It is for people who feel blocked by circumstances, substances, behaviors, attitudes, or beliefs and wonder if this is all there is. Your medicine bag will help you move beyond those internal walls and awaken your awareness of possibilities. It will help you uncover and recover your authentic self.

We each put a unique spin on our inner wall. Whether yours says "I'm not good enough," "I don't deserve that," "I'm not worthy," or "Yes, but it's too late . . ." isn't the point. They are all variations on the theme: *I'm not loveable.* They stand between you and your celebration of life. When you make the conscious decision to quiet the self-destructive chorus in your head and tune into Spirit, you will discover your innate value and begin living the truth of who you are.

It Takes What It Takes

We each seek help for a variety of reasons. Often it will be one or more of the following conditions that bring us to the brink: intense feelings of emptiness, abandonment, shame, fear, guilt, loss, confusion, anxiety, anger, and depression. In well-meaning, but misguided, attempts to self-correct the conditions, another layer is often added to the perfect storm brewing inside us. We turned to alcohol and drugs—both the prescription kind and the back-alley kind. Or we made our own drug out of compulsive and mindless activities like shopping, eating or not eating, bingeing and purging, gambling, technology, sex, work, or (add your fix to the list). These distractions grow until at some point the "cure" becomes the cause; we feel lost and hopeless. What we don't usually realize at this point and what we are about to discover is that wrapped in that perfect storm is our *perfect wholeness.*

We are born whole and perfect spirits on this human journey. We are curious, imaginative, and brave—perfect even in our imperfection.

Life can take a chunk (or more) out of us, or at least it appears to do that. However, in the face of overwhelming circumstances—both self-inflicted mistreatment and that which we receive from others—part of our spirit shuts down. It hides out and stays hidden until we get to a time in our life when we can heal from whatever has gotten us off course. The real gift of recovery is in discovering that your spirit has survived intact, whole, and perfect. As we come to this awareness, our hopes and dreams are energized and we are comforted in our serenity.

You Are What You Believe You Are

Most recovery programs spend a lot of time focused on the broken parts. After the initial healing, this focus tends to reinforce the problem. We need information to help us understand what we are facing and develop helpful strategies on how to do "it" differently ("it" being life as we are meant to live it). We need help in discovering who we are—*really are*—beneath all the programming and adaptations we have used to get where we are.

Abstaining from our substance or behavior is the essential first layer in a successful recovery, but we can't live life from *not doing* something. Life draws us forward, and it works best when we are moving toward something that grabs our attention, speaks our language, and calls our name. Stopping short of finding our dream and pursuing it jeopardizes our attempts at sobriety, and, all too often, our best efforts only result in more best efforts. That's why *Spirit Recovery Medicine Bag* encourages you to find your thing—whatever that might mean for you—and go for it. It offers insightful information and practices for awakening the happy, joyous, and free life inside you. They are offered in the spirit of suggestions with the recovery axiom "Take what you like and leave the rest." As you will see, we believe in choice and responsibility for your choices as a principle of life. Now on with the story.

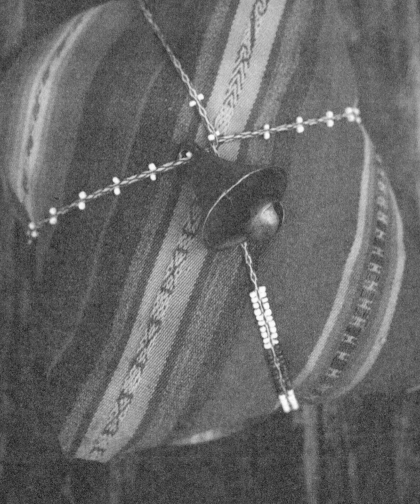

Part One

LEE'S STORY: EXPECT A MIRACLE

A Note From Lee

This is my personal journey of recovery and transformation. These ten-year-old reflections share my realization that my life was about living a story rather than about living an authentic life, and what it took to wake me up. If I were to write these words today, my story might read quite differently, but it wouldn't be true to my experiences as I lived them. We get well. We grow. We change. We can never step into the same river twice, and the same is true of life.

Before I woke up, my reality was always about the beliefs I had formed based on the past. Anything new was filtered through those beliefs, and it all began to look a lot alike . . . too much alike. Being me had become a difficult experience. Something deep inside me knew that my life had no good reason for being difficult and that I had no good reason for not being satisfied. I could no longer justify my situation; it didn't make sense anymore. That was not easy to admit, but, all in all, getting honest was the greatest gift I could have given myself.

CHAPTER 1

Time to Wake Up

"My name is Lee, and I'm an addict."

That is how I used to refer to myself, and, for a long time, it was how I defined myself. I was never comfortable with that definition. I suffered from an addiction, but I was more than that addiction.

What is recovery? What are we recovering to or from? What's the point? These are questions I've asked others and myself as my personal recovery unfolded. In the beginning, there came a point at which I needed help with the chaos of my life. I was told that I suffered from an incurable disease and that this chronic condition could kill me at any time. I was not "normal." I was an addict. Being addict meant I was either in recovery or I was living in my disease. I was either doing it right or I was doing it wrong.

I was also told that, on a deeper level, I suffered from emotional dysfunction. Guilt, shame, and fear were feeding my addiction. I was out of touch with my feelings and my emotional responses to those feelings. My emotions and emotional reactions were way out of line with what might actually be happening in the moment. I was over-reactive and overwhelmed. Being addicted was a setup for using drugs to deal with all my exaggerated emotional reactions. Because I suffered from this disease, I resorted to medicators instead of processing my feelings. I lived in a state of fear of my disease and hopelessness because I was powerless over that disease. I was also powerless over my reactions. I lived a cycle of emotion, reaction, and using that spun faster and faster, feeding on itself.

The case made by the recovery professionals was compelling and scary. There was no way out. I could do everything that was "suggested" and learn to live with all this stuff, or I was destined to end up dead, in prison, or insane.

Stop! All I want is to be happy.

In this world, happiness is a tall order. Happy had to be earned; it was something I did not deserve until I had fulfilled all of the requirements. I had been taught that I wasn't good enough unless I lived up to all the expectations of all the people I cared about. Being good enough was a prerequisite to being happy. This became my belief. That belief was a lie. What I had to earn was the right to believe in myself and in my decisions, if for no other reason than because my life was the sum of my choices, and it belonged to only me.

The first obstacle to happiness was my belief in needing to fit in. The belief that fitting in would bring happiness made me inauthentic. From that point forward, I sought validation from the world that I was good enough. I became a chameleon—changing my look, my talk, and my angle depending on whomever I was with or where I was. Just being me was not good enough. I had to be bigger and better.

What I wanted was peace and a resolution of the fear and insanity in my life. Admitting that I was insane and that my life had become unmanageable was the first step. I didn't have to agree with everything to get what I needed in the moment. The initial answer was in my willingness to accept help. I wasn't finished trying to figure things out, but I could see that I needed some help. My shell of personal importance had cracked. Maybe I didn't have to have all the answers. Maybe I could stand to learn a thing or two.

✦ ✦ ✦

To unravel our lives, we must begin at the beginning. We have to work our way into our core and back out again. In our core, we keep our deepest, most sacred beliefs and agreements. Some of those are so old and are buried so deep that we've lost awareness of them. They have become secrets we keep from ourselves.

CHAPTER 2

The One in the Mirror

Expect a Miracle.
That's what the sign read as we turned onto the road to the treatment center.

"Expect a Miracle." *Do I need a miracle? Hell yes! Hell no! I'm fine. Hah! You're crazy! That's what you are—sick, sick, sick. Boy, you really did it this time.*

I felt like a hero and a fool.

What am I doing here?

I was scared. When you've lived your life in a maze of secrets and lies, getting honest is terrifying. My mask of cool had just turned to mud. Then I remembered: *I am so tired of feeling like shit. I am so tired of being who I have become. Maybe I am in the right place. God, I hope so.*

There was a sense of freedom in knowing how broken-down I was. It was actually a relief. I had left behind miserable relationships, lawsuits, nightmares, and broken hearts.

Expect a miracle? You bet! If it's miracles you're offering, I could sure use one.

✦ ✦ ✦

So the cowboy went into treatment. I got bled, weighed, and medicated. I was interviewed, assessed, and assigned. At some point during those first few days, I was told that if I could surrender—if I would let go and let God—I could learn to live happy, joyous, and free.

I clearly remember my intake interview. Sandy, the intake counselor, asked a lot of questions I thought I had already answered prior to admission, but she was really nice to look at, so I had no problem going over my story again. As I sat in her office, I remember thinking, *What a babe, and what a dumb position for me to be in when I'd much rather be talking to her about how we might hook up.* Then I remembered why I was there, and suddenly, Mr. Cool was put in his place. She was my first real conversation in treatment, and, as I looked in her eyes, I felt like maybe this was where I was supposed to be.

As my interview came to a close she said, "I lived in Nashville for several years. I can give you the names of some recovering people there who you could connect with when you return home." She also made it a point to say, "The journey you're embarking on isn't easy, but you're worth it, so hang in there."

I thanked her and said, "I just want to be happy—happy, joyous, and free."

Sandy's offer was real and sincere. I walked out of her office feeling like there was hope. I was told a lot of stuff and given all kinds of information, but nothing stuck with me as much as "happy, joyous, and free."

I entered a community of people who were joined by their woundedness. We were refugees of an emotional and spiritual war. My reality had become a hell of guilt, shame, fear, misery, and addiction—not much of a party. We all had one thing in common: We couldn't get along with ourselves, the one in the mirror. There were all kinds of stories, all kinds of horrible experiences. There were addicts, codependents, anorexics, and alcoholics. There were incest survivors, self-mutilators, psychotics, and the depressed. There was every manifestation of hate, fear, and misery imaginable.

When I arrived at the Tucson airport a few days earlier, the transportation coordinator was there to greet me. He tried to make me feel welcome and said that there was another client arriving in a few minutes. "As soon as she gets in, we can make the drive to the treatment center," he assured me.

When I close my eyes, I can still see the stranger's face as she approached our driver. She was terrified. I had seen fear before but never that kind of terror. During our stay in treatment, this stranger and I got to be friends. As her story unfolded, I understood the fear in her eyes. She had watched her father, a respected professor at a Colorado university, beat and abuse her mother until one day he left her in a coma on their kitchen floor. When her dad left the house to get a drink at a local bar, she had called an ambulance. After that episode, she began to binge drink and tried to kill herself, before finally seeking help in treatment.

Another friend I made in treatment was a well-known musician who had the reputation of being an out-of-control sex, drugs, and rock-'n'-roller. Most people's opinions of him were based on blind judgments and resentment. I learned that several years before he had watched his baby girl die of cancer. He watched her die, and there was *nothing* he could do about it. He told me one night while we were sitting outside looking up at the desert sky that he hadn't been able to really give a shit about anything since, so he drank Jack Daniels and declared war on the world. The loneliness in his voice broke my heart. There was nothing I could say but "I'm sorry" and even that felt empty.

Among all of us in treatment, our lowest common denominator was our relationship with ourselves, with our suffering, and with our fear. We didn't trust, we didn't believe, and we didn't know what to do to change the hell we were living in.

And so began my process of waking up to the truth of the relationship I had created with life on earth. It was time. I was done with the way my life had been.

CHAPTER 3

Bigger Than Life

I grew up in the shadow of a man I believed ruled a kingdom far greater than Avalon; he was my dad. His name was Benjamin, Captain Ben. That's what the old-timers called him, *Captain Ben*. He was born in 1907 in a little cracker town in Florida. His grandparents—a pair of real pioneers—settled on the property under the homestead law during the Civil War.

My mom was raised in Tennessee, Alabama, and Neptune Beach, Florida. She met my dad in Florida. Daddy used to say that Nanny, my mom's mom, was the meanest white woman he ever met. And it wasn't his style to exaggerate. When I was a kid growing up, my Nanny lived in Neptune Beach. My mom and I would go visit her; my dad always had something else he needed to do.

Nanny was sweet to me, but for some reason, she was hell on almost everybody else. By the time I was ten years old, she was getting in trouble chasing people out of her yard and down the street with a

16

two-by-four with nails sticking out of it. At ten that was funny to me. Nobody else thought so, so she was moved into a nursing home. As I see it, she was fed up with the world she lived in and dealt with it the best way she knew how. For many of us, that frustration leads to addictions or doctor-prescribed medication. For Nanny it was, "Leave me the f—k alone." I wish they had done just that.

My dad was the boss. He ran the family-owned construction company. That was a big job. As general contractors, the company built everything from Highway A1A down the east coast of Florida in the 1930s: pouring all the concrete for the runways and launch pads at Cape Canaveral, and building air bases in Vietnam and dams in South Carolina. My dad's company was also the primary contractor for SeaWorld and Disney's Epcot Center in Orlando. Whatever was going on, my dad was in the middle of it. He didn't watch; he worked. He led by example. If you insulted him or any of his people (and that meant anybody on his payroll), then you had him to deal with, and that was no joke. One man who had worked for my dad his entire life told me that, if my father couldn't whip you the first time, there would be a second time—and you could count on that.

I got some of my dad's determination. I may not punch someone out for looking at me the wrong way, but when I decide to do something, I don't quit.

I was named after Grandpa Lee, my mom's dad. He was a teacher and coach and had been sheriff in Sand Mountain, Alabama. I never knew him, but I always felt close to him. When I was a kid, my mother's side of the family always told me that I was gentle like Grandpa Lee. Being named after him gave us a connection. Now that I have a granddaughter, I understand that connection and the responsibility of leaving behind a legacy to be proud of. Although I never knew my grandfather Lee, I love him anyway. I always felt like he was around and that he could hear me when I talked to him.

My brother, Skip, was fourteen years old when I was born. He was bigger than life. When I was a little boy, I would sit for hours, looking out the front window and waiting for him to come home from college. He was a cross between John Belushi in *Animal House* and Burt Reynolds in *Smokey and the Bandit*. He was my hero, and I loved him. My favorite thing as a kid was going to the Surf-Maid Drive-In with Skip and eating French fries. He drove a candy-apple red '57 Chevy. That was "The Ride," and I was his proud little brother.

Skip had been the center on his high school football team and had a college scholarship until he tore a ligament in his knee. From that point on, his life became about *what could have been if only.* . . . He did his best to live up to the expectations of being my father's oldest son. In his own eyes, I don't think he ever felt good enough, so he lived a pattern of sabotaging himself. There always seemed to be some wreck just waiting to happen where Skip was involved. The family arguments and battles that resulted from Skip's mishaps left me sad and just wanting to be left alone. At the age of fifty-four, Skip died of a prescription-drug overdose. I know it was an accident, and I also know that accidents like that are a long time coming.

My sister, Barbara, served as a "translator" between my father and me, but, being sixteen years older than I was, she was married and gone from home by the time I was five. My dad was forty-nine when I was born, and those forty-nine years were the difference between horses and buggies and going to the moon. I needed an interpreter, but I no longer had my sister to count on. She was always up to her ears in her own problems. She had an affinity for drunks. She liked to marry them and then try to make it work. Today they call that type of relationship *codependency*, a setup for misery for all involved—adults, children, dogs, and cats. It is an energetic nightmare. I love my sister, but we've never had anything other than genetics and drama in common.

✦ ✦ ✦

I grew up on the beach in Florida. If you had asked me then who I was, I would have answered "Ben's son" or "a McCormick." Being a McCormick was larger than life. Because I was a McCormick, everything would be okay. You see, in my little Southern beach hometown, my grandparents on my dad's side had built the first two-story house. That house was a landmark in Jacksonville Beach. In the late sixties, it was sold and torn down to make way for the first McDonald's in the area. I was there with my mom and dad just before the demolition, and as a kid, I could feel the end of an era hanging in the air. That house had been headquarters for an entire tribe of people. All the lives that had been lived there breathed life into those walls. The tearing down of that landmark introduced me to the turning of the tide in our personal history. The feeling was like a footnote I would revisit many times over the coming years.

My grandfather had been the boss, and when he died, he'd passed that power on to my dad. My uncles were pretty powerful, too: One had been mayor for a spell, and another the chief of police. The McCormicks weren't into money and glamour; they were cracker-pioneer, sweat-blood, and get-the-job-done kind of people. Life was hard, and they were harder. I must have heard ten thousand times growing up, "Git up, git with it, or git out of my way!" I tried to be "their way," but I couldn't make it work. I believed I was less than. After all, a man was a man, and, in the presence of those proud, no-holds-barred men, I felt like a mouse. I learned early on how to be sly. I had never learned to trust who I am—the one inside this body, the one who had a whole life out in front of him. I never figured out who I was, me, Lee.

I lived life doing what I loved: surfing or staying at our family's farm—the one that my great-grandparents homesteaded—hunting, fishing, riding my horse, going with my dad to check the cows. I've lived all over the United States, and I've never known a more magical place than the cypress ponds and blackwater swamps of Florida. I can feel it right now: thick humid heat and the buzzing of mosquitoes. The "skeeters" got so thick that the cows bunched up as tight as they could, swishing their tails, trying to keep from getting bled out by the bugs.

Having grown up on a farm with all that life moving around me, the smells and sounds, the changing seasons, and the life and death a hair's breadth away left a deep imprint on me. All those old-timers had such respect and love for the woods and the animals. I was taught never to kill anything you don't eat. I was also taught that there was a place in the natural world for all creatures and that creation is bigger than us and we've got to respect that.

We ran cattle in the woods, but my dad was always careful to not overgraze so that there would be feed for the deer and turkeys. The men dug water holes that, in droughts, were a refuge for the gators and turtles and the only source of drinking water for the wildlife as well as the cattle. These men had an awareness of balance, knowing it was to be respected and protected. We'd all ride through the farm on my dad's extended WWII Willis Jeep, checking the condition of the pastures and the cattle. Deer, wild turkeys, wild hogs, and armadillos dotted the landscape wherever we looked. On the weekends, one of my uncles and his family (and some of the other members of my dad's company tribe) would come out and we'd work cows or catch hogs for bacon and sausage. While the men worked, us kids would swim in the clear cold lake in front of the house, which was fed by a huge artesian well. Though there was a 'gator now and then, that lake was our refuge from the heat.

The scene was idyllic and everything would seem great ... that is, till my dad and uncle would get into an argument over some business bullshit. When they squared off, the atmosphere of the entire 5,000-acre farm would shift from heaven to hell. As I've said before, my people were tough. They took offense to being challenged or disrespected. If you pushed too hard or said something out of line, you'd better be ready to back it up.

All that frustration and anger was exhausting, and it scared the shit out of me as a little kid. I learned to create my own secret places where I couldn't hear them and where I could be alone with the magic of the woods. I favored the swamps and the cypress ponds. Spirits dwell in those places where the shadows are long, and something's always moving out of the corner of your eye. Among those palmettos and oaks, I'd spy deer and squirrels, and once, I'd even seen a panther. I'd pretend to be invisible and that I could sneak up on the animals and get close enough to touch them.

I loved being in the presence of the animals. They were surrounded by peace, magic, and mystery. In the mystery, I was free from the need to be good enough or correct. The mystery touched something inside me that was deep and clear like a cold clean spring of awareness, pure life without all the baggage of the adult human world.

CHAPTER 4

The Trip

I never wanted to grow up. What I saw from grownups was a mess of arguments, struggle, pressure, and divorce. During those years at the farm, the friction between my parents grew intense. My mom wanted to enjoy the beauty of our world, while my dad was buried under the pressure of being responsible for everything in that world. I remember lying in bed at night, hearing them argue until it turned into an all-out fight. I hated the meanness and anger, all the poison they put on each other. Listening to it made me feel sick. The adult world looked (and especially felt) like a war zone. *Screw that!* I may not have known who I was, but I damn sure knew what I didn't want to be. If being an adult was what I saw going on, I was not interested.

My mother had a strong heart and needed it every step of the way. Destiny married her to two men who walked tall and carried big sticks. In this world, like attracts like, so all I can figure is that, if my mom had been a man, she would have been an equal to both the men she married. She did her best at everything she did. I'd seen her stand her ground with my dad and my stepdad when anyone else would have backed down. She never acted out of meanness; she just wouldn't compromise her integrity.

My mother grew up on Sand Mountain in Alabama. She picked cotton as a child and lived through the Depression. I expect she found a way to make it all not so bad. Some people live through hard times and come out addicted to suffering, while others come out glad that it is over and ready to move on. That's her, always looking up and out.

My stepdad's name was Artemis Darius, or A.D. for short. My mom married him in 1970. Although my parents' divorce had devastated me, having A.D. as a stepdad was cool with me; I had known him all my life. He was a bit intimidating and way intense, but I liked him. It was A.D.'s way or no way. I liked that attitude, but I never had the guts to carry it through like he did. I loved A.D., but I never shared that with him until his last stay in the hospital.

Anyway, our connection was never about conversation. A.D. liked action, and so did I. When I reached "adulthood," we became partners in the cattle business; I invested my energy and he invested his money. I spent a couple of years working on his ranches, learning the ropes of the cattle-feeding business, and, when I was just getting comfortable, he made me a partner and told me he wanted 10,000 head of cattle on feed before the end of the year. To put this in perspective, I felt like a guy who had just made it to assistant manager of a Wal-Mart, then Sam Walton calls and says, "Hey! You're my new partner, and you're responsible for the future of this company."

The learning curve was a bitch, but I was determined to make it work. If I could be "good enough" for A.D. Davis, well then the devil could kiss my ass. I started buying cattle and leasing ranches. Within five years, we had 5,000 cows between our ranches in Tennessee and South Florida. In addition, we were keeping several thousand cattle on feed in feedlots from Iowa to Texas. A.D. had gotten me connected to trading cattle and grain futures, which turned out to be a game I had an affinity for. Like I said earlier, he liked action and so did I.

But that was later.

✦ ✦ ✦

I started playing guitar and smoking reefer when I was fifteen. Guitars and surfboards went hand in hand, and I loved both. There is something sweet about spending the days surfing and getting fried in the sun, then taking a cold shower and heading back to the beach to pick and sing with your buddies and of course the girls. Tan lines and coconut oil made our world go around. Being a teenage boy was a grand experience. Girls were such a mystery and so beautiful and soft to touch. When I was fifteen, I had my first intimate girlfriend. She was sixteen and had a car, so life was killer. She also surfed. Sex was something that was too alluring to resist and to be in the water with your too-cute girlfriend, the attraction was better than any drug ever—before or since.

A buddy of mine had a beach house an hour south in St. Augustine and his parents were out of town one weekend; the waves were good and my girlfriend had a great excuse for her parents and so did I. We took off after school, drove south, surfed till dark, and got lost in each other all night. At dawn, we were back in the waves. Life might get bigger and more interesting and it grows in meaning and experience, but it doesn't get any sweeter—not until you share babies together, and that's a whole other story.

Smoking grass was part of our culture. Back then it was easy to get a bag of pot—much easier than getting someone to buy alcohol for us. Anyway, alcohol left me feeling like shit. These days the scene has gotten really ugly around meth and other hard-core poisons, but there's always somebody smoking a joint at the beach and watching the surf. To tell you the truth, I've got no agenda against it ... unless it becomes an excuse to not live life.

After Mom and A.D. got married, I moved into my dad's leased house overlooking the ocean. I could check the waves every day from my bedroom window. After high school I went to college, all the way to Colorado. I still had no idea who I was, and that made me a little afraid. College meant partying, playtime, getting stoned, and going skiing. Life was becoming about go-go-go! By now I was hardwired for not doing anything I didn't want to do. I was afraid I might get trapped in that miserable world of adult insanity. I wondered why people stayed where they were in life if they were so unhappy. College was fun and challenging.

Years of playing music on the beach evolved into my first paying gig at a Shakey's Pizza in Durango, Colorado. I'd become friends with a guy in college who had played a few gigs before, so we teamed up and found our chance at Shakey's. Those Thursday nights were a dream come true—free pizza and beer, forty dollars cash, and all that attention from the ladies. Durango was a small town of around 15,000 people with 3,000 students at Fort Lewis College. The college's claim to fame was all the people they had put on the U.S. Olympic ski team.

It's a funny aside now, but our local ski area was Purgatory ... a place I'd get to know on many levels as time moved on. From Bob Dylan and Dan Fogelberg to the Eagles, Cat Stevens, and CSNY—the music was a perfect soundtrack to the life I was dreaming. Living in the Rockies, I traded in my surfboard for skis and snowshoes. I had found freedom in a place where nobody knew my dad or any of my family. There were all kinds of characters and beautiful women to fuel my adventures.

The stillness of the high country after a new snow was the same great magical mystery that I had touched on in the swamps of home years before. One weekend I was asked to come out to Wolf Creek

Inn and play since their regular guy had run off with the owner's wife. Wolf Creek was one of the premier powder havens in the West. There was a great local crowd, and as the night progressed, the assistant manager, who happened to be hot and single, offered me a line of the other powder. I wasn't a coke addict then, but I also wasn't afraid, so I followed her to the backroom and before long we were in the hot tub together and the music was over for the night. *Crank up the stereo, boys, we're going for sunrise.*

I left college and started playing music professionally. I loved it. I played honky-tonks and bars from Albuquerque to St. Augustine. By this time, the menu of mind-altering substances had expanded—from smoking weed to occasional mushrooms and Quaaludes. I didn't feel a "need" to get high back then; it was just part of the culture—all that young and wild acting out stuff my generation did back then. From '74 to '79, I lived back and forth between the Rockies and the beach. When the ski season ended and the spring semester was over, I'd plug in Bob Marley or Jimmy Buffet and drive east until Interstate-10 dead-ended into the Atlantic Ocean. In the fall, the trail back would meander through New Orleans, where I'd always find a place to play for a week, then on to Texas, through the panhandle, and back to the Rockies and the first snow. Packing up and heading out, whether it was from Durango to Florida or Florida back to Durango, was always bittersweet—a feeling that has remained with me throughout my life. In fact, over the years since I've moved beyond living with an addiction as my traveling companion, my heartfelt connection to places that I love brings up that old "Don't really want to leave, but I love where I'm headed" kind of feeling.

One year, just before I left the beach to head for Durango, one of my close girlfriends asked me if I'd give her big sister a ride to Durango. When she brought her sister into the room, I went stupid; she was beautiful and had been a professional ballet dancer who'd blown out her knee. I couldn't believe she was going to be driving across country with me. *Oh man . . . so how many nights could we stretch this out?* She was sweet enough to love me a little but made it clear she had other business once we got to Durango. All good. I was in love for some time, though, and spent a lot of time hanging out in the restaurant she worked at in Durango.

Life was a great adventure, and I was open to whatever came next. The world was a mystery to me. I had no real sense that life could be hard or even have serious consequences. I loved living and traveling— going one day from beach life to honky-tonk havens and cowboy culture the next. For a kid who had talent enough to make a living playing music and who also had family support behind him, I was a free bird. Beautiful scenery, an open road, a world full of beautiful girls, and buddies to run with—there was nothing but the moment . . . and the next. I had never seen the dark side of life, so I didn't realize I was playing on the edge of a world I hadn't yet experienced. I had no idea the temptations of the shadow lands were about to fall right in my lap.

✦ ✦ ✦

During the summer of '77 I connected with the one relationship I couldn't leave behind. She had my number the night we finally met up close and personal. What started as the hottest affair I'd ever had ended by showing me the gates of hell. She was the angel of death, the Peruvian princess: cocaine.

Our formal introduction came on a Saturday night. One of my best friends had a buddy who had been a Special Forces soldier in Vietnam. Since the war ended he worked as a merchant sailor between the United States and South America. He told us stories of the side jobs he would get from U.S. agents in South America. Then they would fly him back to the United States on military planes, no customs, and he'd stash a kilo of coke in his luggage. On that Saturday night, he'd just gotten back from Colombia, and the coke was as pure as it gets. We all sat around a big dining-room table passing a plate full of powder and talking like an auctioneer's convention. The next thing I knew, it was Sunday morning and I was bulletproof. My affair with the lie had begun.

Some lessons in life may come easy, but I don't remember them. I was raised to believe that life was a struggle, one continuous battle of the will. But I thought I had avoided the trap of that belief system. What I didn't realize was that, by believing life was a struggle, I was going to live a struggle, regardless of how cool my lifestyle might have appeared.

In '78 I moved to Nashville. I had played music all over the country. After being told a thousand times, "You should go to Nashville," I went. Nashville in the late seventies was a great scene. I spent most of the next couple of years on the road—sex, drugs, and country music. Waylon Jennings had a great bumper-sticker quote: "This is the big time. There are no dress rehearsals. We are professionals." That was it, nonstop.

I lived so fast in Nashville that I burnt out. The music business was a bizarre combination of talent, creativity, and balls-to-the-wall endurance. We would go on the road for a month, playing small concert halls, big bars, and music festivals. We worked a great giant honky-tonk in Tuscaloosa, Alabama, called Lee's Tomb. That place held 300 people, and we'd pack it. Wild, drunk, crazy college students and Alabama's finest old hippies would come together to listen and party. From there we'd go to Florida or Chicago. The road went on forever, and the party never ended.

Everywhere we went after every show, it was the same routine: The locals wanted to party, and we were quick to take them up on it. Sometime around sunup we'd head back to the hotel, sleep for a few hours, and head down the road to do it all over again. I still felt no attachment to the drugs—it was just something we did from place to place. I was beginning to realize, though, that there were things I'd do high that I wouldn't do sober.

Finally one day I looked in the mirror, and what I saw scared the shit out of me. I'd just turned twenty-four, but a man twice my age was staring back at me. *Time to take a break.*

CHAPTER 5

Not Showing Up

In 1980 I went back to college and graduated with a major in business and minors in theater, agriculture, and music. My interests were (and are) diverse, and college had become a place to investigate all my real interests. Being in school was also a refuge from the official world—besides, when you don't really know who you are, it's good to have a lot of masks. I continued to party, but I was managing to keep it together. During this time, I met the woman who would become my first wife. We were a great match; she had no more idea who she was than I did. Her aspiration in life was to be a West Nashville country-club princess. She was well on her way until her boyfriend ate too many Quaaludes and wrapped his car around a tree; he never woke up again. We had been hanging out together at school at the time and her heartbreak opened the door for our rebound engagement.

Just before we got married, she told her dad she wanted out of the wedding, and he told her she'd come too far to back out now. Not long after we were married she told me I could never be what her ex had been to her, and, if he'd been alive, she would have never married me. Well, there isn't much to say to that. I could have walked, and I didn't. I guess I hoped somehow it would all work out. Anyhow, we were both trying to find a way to fit into this new relationship and the world of expectations, all at the same time. It was a bit much.

We were twenty-something adolescents, doing what all good red-blooded American kids are supposed to do. We expected marriage to work like we had been told. It didn't. My attachment to getting high had grown, and I became restless. I started to look for women to do coke with. I didn't like doing it alone, and, for me, coke and women went hand in hand. This was a double-barreled betrayal of my marriage and myself.

So, our marriage didn't work, but we did have two beautiful daughters together. When my first daughter was born, I learned what true love felt like. I had experienced feelings that I thought were love, but they weren't. Holding that little girl touched a part of me that remembered the truth of life. She was my baby, and my love for her was unconditional. Of course *talking love* and *being love* are two different things. I had no idea of the distance between "my saying" and "my doing." Being a coke addict created a blind spot in my entire being that separated my perception from any semblance of truth or accuracy. As empty as it sounds, my addicted mind would accept what I wanted to do as good enough when what I was doing was lying and not showing up for the people in my life who really mattered. My mind accepted good intentions as if good intentions had some great value.

In time, we moved from Nashville to my stepdad's ranch in Colorado for a year, then on to Florida. I made a connection with myself, working on A.D.'s ranch. I lived, ate, and breathed cowboying. The Ranch was straight out of the old days. The cowboys lived in a bunkhouse, and we all ate in the cookhouse. First bell on a regular day was 5:00 AM; breakfast was at 6:00. There were 1,200 cows spread out on a hundred thousand acres of northern Colorado paradise. We'd catch our horses right after breakfast and be in the saddle by 7:00 AM. The ranch was twelve miles across and twenty miles long, and my butt covered every section of it. I was so happy there that looking for blow and getting high were no longer a priority. Still, I knew it was around.

I loved my wife and our life as a family on the Ranch. It was a flashback of my childhood where the really happy times had been on our farm in Florida or out at my dad's ranch in Wyoming. Those were the connected, sweet places where my family's intensity didn't bleed through for me as a kid. Living there was that old dream come back to life.

One evening I went home and told my wife how I felt like I was living on a movie set. She didn't share my love for the West, so the movie thing was lost on her. She told me that all the cowboys in that town looked alike, walked alike, and talked alike, and what she wanted was a house in Denver where the men wore suits and didn't smell like large animals. My reply was that all those businessmen in Denver looked alike, walked alike, and talked alike, as far as I could tell, and I preferred large animals to cocktail parties.

The writing was on the wall.

You don't do ranch work for the money; you do it because you love it. I would never want just a job. Life is too short not to live what you love. My wife didn't love it; she decided she was moving back to Nashville. She told me later she never expected I would follow her, but I did. I followed my little girl.

Moving back to Tennessee was exciting and uncomfortable. By this time I had a big inventory of frustrations, resentments, and guilt. Our marriage was starting to feel like a trap. I felt like I was not good enough and had plenty of opportunities to prove it to my wife and to myself. My wife said, more than once, that I was not who she'd have married had she not been pressured by her family. There were a lot of things said that should have ended our marriage. Nevertheless, we stayed with it for thirteen years. During that time, I gradually took more and more refuge in that old relationship with Coca, the Queen of Lies. What once had been fun and wickedly cool had become a habit.

For the first few years, doing coke was a take-it-or-leave-it situation. I can't tell you when I crossed that line from indulgence to addiction. The deeper I got into that life, the more my lack of personal awareness and personal responsibility sabotaged my happiness. I believed what I had been taught all my life, that we are what we do and how well we do it.

Who we are and what we do are two different things. I believed I was less than, because I was not good enough to make it work. I was mad at me; I was mad at my wife. I was afraid of not living up to everybody's expectations. So I got high as often as possible.

As this evolved, I worked with A.D., creating a ranching and cattle-feeding operation in Tennessee. I was doing exactly what I wanted. The ranch was beautiful, and the intensity of the cattle and commodities markets was a perfect fix for me. My life looked like a dream come true. In truth, it was a slow-ticking time bomb.

When you're a coke addict, you learn that if you're going to show up for your responsibilities you have to fake feeling okay. Staying up all night doing dope and drinking, then getting to the barn at six in the morning and working all day will make anyone feel old quick. I would do my insane best to not party the nights before we had to work early the next day, but being addicted has something to say about when and where I'd do whatever.

I still remember driving home as the sun rose, actually believing the lies I was going to tell about where I'd been and what I'd been doing. My answer to being so out of control was to do more of everything.

Lease more ranches, so I could travel more, so I could be away from home more, so I could get high and chase women more.

Meanwhile the job I was doing was shit. I put responsibilities on people that were more than they were hired for. There were days when I'd have a large position in the commodities market and missing a phone call would cost me thousands of dollars. Of course my wife didn't believe anything coming out of my mouth, so she started making her own plans. It is amazing today that this situation had such a long fuse.

The more I did, the more A.D. wanted to do. We expanded our operation to ranches in Florida, and cattle-feeding arrangements in Iowa, Texas, Kansas, and Missouri. My second daughter was born.

Both of my daughters grew up around the Ranch and the cattle. They had ponies and loved to go with me to move cows or just check pastures, the same way I had loved doing those things with my dad and my stepdad. That was one of those legacies that tied the generations together. If my dad said he was going to do something, he did it; the same was true for A.D. and my mom. They always did their best to do what they believed to be the right thing. I started out practicing that integrity, but the deeper I got into my addiction, the greater my struggle with my own guilt became. The less dependable I was, the more I'd resort to getting high.

This had nothing to do with my wife or daughters. This is the progression of what a lot of people call the disease of addiction. I'm not much on that disease idea, but there is a definite increase in what one might call symptoms—mainly the lying, seeking refuge with women who'd do the drugs with me, and getting lost in obsessing on getting loaded until I'd miss appointments or school functions so that I could write it off and go get loaded. I can't imagine understanding how twisted a life of addiction is if you've never been there. I also see no need in understanding it. Why would anyone want to?

As much as I loved my little girls, I couldn't always make that love more important than my need to get high. Once I started getting high, I sure as hell couldn't stop just because I was supposed to be somewhere with them, so I did the best I could and didn't show up. Showing up high was worse to me than not showing up at all.

Looking back, it's all so weird that it took so long for someone to look me straight in the face and say, "You're an addict and you need help," but that was still a few years off. So I did what I did, and they had to live with it. That sucks, but that's the way it is when kids live with addicted parents. I gave them a lot of stuff and tried to rationalize all the insanity, but in the end it was all one big mess. I did that to me, to my wife, and to my babies.

I broke their hearts.

I can forgive myself for that, but I won't pretend that it was okay. My wife tried her best, and she also made it clear that I had taken her life hostage and I was guilty for her unhappiness. At some point, I got sick of her playing the victim and said f—k it. I never had much use for martyrs. Every time she complained about losing her old happy life, being married to the girls and me, I'd want to explode or go get loaded. Getting loaded was more my style. We were locked into a cycle of sadness and frustration, and neither one of us knew how to stop it.

CHAPTER 6

My Refuge in Hell

Life, I guess, had watched this slow disintegration long enough. My wife filed for divorce while I was in Florida, shipping cattle. I flew back to Nashville to find divorce papers taped to my pickup window. I couldn't breathe. I still carried all the heartbreak of my parents' divorce. And here it was again. Reading my soon-to-be-ex-wife's letter, I wanted to throw up.

When I was twelve, my parents sent me to camp for the summer. I didn't want to go; even at twelve, something about the setup felt wrong. I remember walking in on conversations between my parents and they would stop talking or the subject would change, and I would get so angry inside.

At camp the counselor took me into his office one day and explained how complicated adult relationships were, blah, blah, blah . . . I didn't want to hear it. Wherever he was going, my family was none of his f—king business. When my dad came to pick me up, he told me that he and my mom had separated, and I would be living with her. He was so heartbroken that all I could feel was my love for him, and the fear that he would not be all right.

I didn't want to live with my mom. I wanted to live at home, at the beach. Home was home; it was not some strange house in a strange neighborhood forty miles away in another town. My heart was broken, and I was pissed. I felt like everybody was lying to me about how everything was going to be great, and I was such a good boy, and I'd make new friends, and screw them all. Well, that was what flew into my face as I read my wife's Dear Lee letter. That was the first time I became aware of how we carry our old wounds with us. The difference was I was thirty-eight years old and had an addiction that I could use to separate me from the truth. Instead of someone else lying to me, I was now lying to myself.

I turned to my refuge in hell. One thing I could always count on cocaine to do was cut me off from feeling my emotions. She never let me down when it came to that. When feeling me wasn't what I wanted, I could stick my head in a bag of dope and all I'd feel was the dope, until I was done, then I'd feel worse than ever.

✦ ✦ ✦

Two years after my divorce, A.D. had his last stroke. He'd had a stroke eight years earlier, and, by the strength of his will, he made a miraculous comeback. But time had started taking its toll on his body. He died the Sunday before Father's Day. My dad had passed away eight years earlier, on Father's Day. Six months later, my brother died of a prescription overdose. My life hit the fan, big time, and I had nowhere to hide. I fought to hold on to what A.D. and I had created together. His family's attorneys had a different idea, and they had written the will.

The one aspect of money and power that I've found to be consistent is the way they can corrupt the perception of those who have them. When you identify yourself by what you have, you naturally protect your possessions as though they were your life. They have become your identity, your security. This situation is magnified when the world we are surrounded by supports this distorted point of view. Our faith becomes invested in the underlying belief that we are safe because of what we have. The more we have, the safer we believe we are.

Compassion is displaced by greed, and sincerity is lost to personal importance. The reality is, the more we have, the more time and energy it requires to protect and defend those possessions, because we have invested our identity and safety in them.

A.D.'s family's attorneys were dedicated to protecting their assets. My father had told me straight up that there are very few people in this world that, as he put it, "were big enough to handle success." He was right. He also told me most people would do things for money that money's not worth. Life is too short and self-respect too rare a commodity to put a dollar figure on. From my own experience, I can say that is the truth. So when the conflict started over what A.D. wanted versus what the attorneys said was going to happen, I took the path that was closest to the door.

I tried to take refuge in new relationships, but, with like attracting like, my choices were pretty scary. I hooked up with the ones who would have me. My drugging became worse than ever. The cattle market collapsed, and I lost my ass big time. Ranching has never been a sound economic venture; you have to love it, and when you love it, you don't want to let go. Farmers and ranchers are optimists; they live for the life. Paydays are necessary, but they are not the point. So they do all they can to work all ends toward the middle, barely keeping their head above water.

Commodities markets are fickle realities, and ranching is a commodity business. I inherited a million dollars' worth of cattle from A.D.'s estate, and, by the time the estate was settled, those same cattle were worth about half what they were when he died. It's hard to believe someone can inherit a million dollars' worth of anything and a short time later be busted. It was hard for me to believe, and it had happened to me.

Life did what was necessary to get my attention. This wasn't easy, considering my unshakeable relationship with the Peruvian princess. Fortunately, Spirit didn't care, and out of what was the craziest female relationship I had been in yet, I started going to a counselor. My girlfriend's dad was an alcoholic, so she had been around 12-Step programs. She told me I needed to get help. I thought I was in love with her, so I did.

She was beautiful and as crazy as I was. When we first met she was in a relationship with another woman; they were both fun and interesting, so we got to be friends. A short time later they broke up. That was just before her birthday, and I offered to take her out to dinner. Like I said she was beautiful, and I really had no expectation of anything developing between us. We had a great dinner at an oceanfront restaurant, and, walking over to the bar next door afterward for a drink, she asked if I'd like to do some coke; that was a no-brainer.

We spent the rest of the night in an oceanfront hotel room, living out one of those great love-story fantasies. It didn't take long for the fantasy to get real. The complicated aspects of both of our lives invaded the relationship. I was like a hurricane looking for a port to tie up in, and she was black widow stalking her next fly. My new girlfriend was a great match for Señor Loco. We lived the South Florida beach life . . . surfboards, Jet Skis, cocaine, and candlelight. We'd often head to Key West where the gender specifics are a bit blurry, and she could get a good table dance faster than I could.

At some point we decided to get married. *Yeah, right.* Two lunatics must be better than one, so why not? At the time, I really thought I was in love so I wanted to give my girl a nice diamond. An old friend in Nashville was a diamond dealer so I dropped several grand on the counter and left with a beautiful three-carat diamond ring. Before it was all said and done that ring would end up being an object of great contention. After she showed it off to her friends, I thought the reactions were nice but a little strange, like they knew something I didn't. The rest of the story centers on another piece of jewelry, a pendant she wore around her neck that had three nice diamonds on it. When I asked her about it, she told me she'd had it made. That was cool and enough of an explanation for me. Then sometime later one of her old friends asked me if I knew the story behind those diamonds.

"No, I mean I know she had it made," I said.

"Well, big boy, you might want to ask her where the diamonds came from," she replied.

So I did. My fiancée copped this evil grin and said simply, "They're old engagement diamonds. I never give diamonds back."

Suddenly that little pendant looked like a Sioux scalp pole, but, instead of hanging in a tepee, it was hanging around her neck. "Oh man" was about all I had to say, well that and, "That diamond will never join those other scalps—not if I can help it." I eventually had to take her to court to get the ring back. I wouldn't have cared so much about it if she hadn't been so proud of that scalp-pole pendant.

For all of our craziness, we did have a lot of fun. She was the one who got me to take a good long look in the mirror. When Spirit takes hold in your life, amazing things happen. I didn't have a clue about that. All I knew was how to sabotage myself. I had no idea how anything could be different, but I was willing to try.

CHAPTER 7

Hell Is Not a Reality

Lifetimes begin and end in a heartbeat. In a heartbeat, in the course of a moment, life can change. In a heartbeat, experiences and opportunities come and go. My heart was beating fast that day in February 1997, as I pulled onto I–95, headed north to Jacksonville, Florida. Forty years old and feeling old, empty, lonely, and scared, I was going home to tell my mom I needed to go into treatment.

Hello, my name's Lee, and I'm an addict.

I didn't know it then, but I was about to meet the one person who would make the difference in my life. After forty years of living and thirteen years of marriage, after chasing dreams, burying friends, spending fortunes, living on that line between heaven and hell, I was about to come face to face with the one I had missed for so long.

Hey, Brother, I'm you.

Before treatment I had no idea what "emotional baggage" was. I

41

knew about anger, joy, and resentment, but I was clueless about our habit of carrying around guilt, fear, and judgment. As my awareness of self grew, it almost made sense how I got to where I was. Not knowing that I was a time bomb of emotional energy, I had dealt with my feelings by smoking, snorting, drinking, and screwing. When the bullshit stops working for you, you have to make a choice. You can take responsibility for yourself and create your life with awareness, or you can continue to dance to whatever's on the jukebox.

In treatment I spent hours in group therapy, acting out memories and nightmares, moving lifetimes of energy. Shedding the skins of grief, fear, and rage leaves a body feeling—even if for just a moment—free and at peace. If we're lucky, that peace will trigger a deeper memory from before our descent into hell. If we had no memories of before we were miserable, we'd have no perspective by which to judge our situation. The frustration of living an unfulfilling life is anchored in the memory of the truth.

The truth is that life is beautiful. It is amazing and magical. We carry that awareness within. We know the truth; we just have no faith in it. So we live for the world, doing and trying to believe what we're told. The harder we try to serve the world, the farther away we move from our memory of the truth—of who we really are. Like quicksand, the harder we try to break free, the faster we sink. We are born of the kingdom of heaven, and we abandon our birthright for the world of men.

Hell is not a reality; it is an experience of the abandonment of truth. The Bible's description of hell doesn't scare me anymore. My ability to create hell for myself is what scares me. Why would God do to us what we do so miserably and proficiently to ourselves?

What I experienced in healing was an inner knowledge that I live what I choose for myself. What I had lived was the reflection of a much bigger lie. I had done the best I could with the choices, as I perceived them—no fault, no blame. What I was doing was just not working anymore. My problem was not only my behaviors; it was my belief system. My behaviors were merely a reflection of how limited my awareness was. If you asked me who I was, you'd hear all about what I did.

I had no relationship with my spirit. I'd tell you what I thought, not what I felt. I can tell you this, when overwhelmed with life I tried to find something, anything, to fill that emptiness. Because I believed life was hard and unfair, it was. Of course it was; I was the one judging my experiences, and I wasn't going to make myself wrong. We see what we believe of the world, not necessarily what we're looking at. Living in pain, fear, and suffering naturally led to wanting to medicate. The medicating evolved into an addiction.

As I began to see myself as the result of my choices, I realized that I had created my situation and that maybe I could change it. I was responsible for what I believed, and what I believed supported my relationship with life. It was the quality of my life that I was offered the opportunity to take responsibility for. But first I had to uncover me and recover a relationship with myself.

The next decision was a big one: *Am I worth it?* To admit that I was worth it meant I had to accept that I had done it to myself. I had to take responsibility for all the choices I had made. To take responsibility required believing that I could choose again, that my life could be different. To choose to take care of myself, to take the risk of accepting help, was a choice of Spirit.

To choose the way of all those medicators—the blame, guilt, anger, sex, and drugs—was the road already traveled. The choice kept coming back to whether or not I would take responsibility for myself, for my life. I'm not talking about the responsibility of being compliant with the world's demands and judgments. What I was realizing was that I had to take responsibility for the quality and direction of the life I was living, because that life was mine and it was up to me to do what I would with it. I was responsible for my own creation. The key to opening the door of freedom was in learning to let go of the fear of saying, "I am wrong" or "I was wrong." That lesson came as a great gift.

Saying I was wrong pushed those buttons of needing to defend myself or, even bigger, automatically judging myself. Wrong equaled bad, not good enough, failure. Okay, so what? When you step back and see what a mess your life is, the truth of that supports being able to learn how to let go of the scorecard and reach for the next choice: the choice toward creating a life you love rather than continuing to feed a life that's not working for you.

I was coming into a new awareness. What would I do with it? I lived in a community of dedicated victims. I heard it all day long: the war stories, abuse, neglect, and injustice. We wore our diagnoses like badges. Every morning in treatment we were required to attend Community Group right after breakfast. We sat around the perimeter of the meeting hall, sixty-something of us, and checked in. We would state our recovery name, *Lee M.*, and our titles, *addict*, *alcoholic*, *codependent*, *depression*, *sex addict*, *bulimic*, and so on. Then we would state how we felt in that moment.

There was a bizarre camaraderie between those of like afflictions. We found acceptance among our own. That acceptance was the beginning of a support system. We were sick together. What all of us did really well was suffer. But I'd had enough suffering. I was not interested in being my own martyr. Martyrs are fools. Regardless of how sincere their beliefs, they get exactly what they ask for. I was ready for something different. I wanted that "happy, joyous, and free" the 12-Steppers talked about. I wanted out of hell. I wanted freedom.

❖   ❖   ❖

Living in treatment presented an interesting situation. Someone looking in would think the place was a camp resort or Southwestern health spa. Beautiful landscaping surrounded adobe-style buildings, and there was a big community pool. My room was just off the pool area, which I thought was pretty cool.

When I first arrived at the treatment center, I was assigned to the detox ward. This was a medical area in one of the main buildings. There was a group of bedrooms, like hospital rooms—three beds per room with one bathroom. I tried to tell them that I didn't need detox and that I hadn't been high for a week, but they had their rules. When I got to my room in detox, I met the other two guys who were my roommates. One was a Hollywood director who was seriously addicted to pain pills; the other guy was a heroin addict from New York. The first night they were up puking and shuffling around the room like ghosts. Sliding their feet across the floor rather than picking them up and taking a step, they made that smooth slide look like a moonwalk from the Cuckoo's Nest.

Being in the detox ward was big-time spooky. I was sick in my mind, crazy . . . it wasn't physically noticeable unless I'd been up for a couple of days all tweaked out. These new comrades of mine were death walking, and that scared me. I couldn't help but wonder just how bad off I was if this is where I needed to be to get better.

Our first morning together, I walked to breakfast as they stared downward and shuffled to the cafeteria. My attention was all over the place, looking out the windows at the beautiful mountains above the center and around the halls at the other patients. Getting to the breakfast line was a pleasant surprise when I realized the food was actually okay. I really wanted a cup of coffee, but there was no caffeine or sugar allowed on the premises. This is because alcoholics crave sugar to replace the sugar their bodies have become accustomed to from the alcohol. And as far as coffee was concerned, treatment centers aren't interested in stimulating their patients, which is why caffeine wasn't on the menu. We needed to slow down, not speed up.

After two nights in detox, I was moved to my assigned room. I was never more grateful to have my own space away from the nightmare of the continuous flow of newly arriving patients. During my stay in treatment, I saw everything from the shuffling heroin addicts to the tweaked-out speed freaks and crack heads. Some of them would actually sit outside in the parking lot to smoke their last hits of dope before checking in. I couldn't relate to that. When I got high, that was all I was going to do; the rest of the time I was so ashamed and afraid of when I'd get on my next roll. When I made the decision to go to treatment, that was that. I was not going to blow it.

✦ ✦ ✦

Treatment was the beginning of a reeducation in being human. They gave me all kinds of information on the nature and use of medicators. Our society maintains itself with medicators; they are the cornerstones of our civilization. Our economic system thrives on the insatiable American appetite for more. We are taught that if you want respect, you have to be bigger, faster, prettier . . . more. We are taught that fulfillment comes from the outside in. It is what we accomplish that determines our value. The people who can't take any more of that medicate, because they are terrified they'll find out they are the only ones who can't make it work—that it is all their fault.

My treatment was built around a primary group, which was made up of nine people, both male and female, who were grouped by the assessments of the intake department and the clinical team. The center had sixty-something patients, so there were seven or eight primary groups running at a time. Each group met every morning from 9:15 to 10:45. The first morning in primary, I walked in to see a guy I had met years before in Jacksonville, my old hometown. He was part of an iconic Southern rock band, and I'd played with one of his old band mates at some clubs in Jacksonville. We'd met while partying after a show. It amazed me that all those years later, halfway across the country, I walked into a group in a treatment center and there sat somebody I knew. It made the world seem small.

The group process was built around open sharing and a process known as psychodrama. Psychodrama is a spontaneous process where the individual doing the work talks through an unresolved situation in his or her life. The person of focus identifies the people or aspects of the situation that he or she wants to work on, and, with the guidance of the therapist, the other members of the primary group are assigned roles to represent those people or things. Like a magical theater, the therapist guides the group into a re-creation of the dynamics that live on in that person's memory and stored emotions.

Participating in a support role was almost as, and sometimes just as, powerful an experience as being in the lead role. On one occasion, I was asked to play a group mate's deceased father. I took a place on the floor as if I were in a casket at my funeral and a sheet was placed over me. My group mate's dad had drunk himself to death a few years earlier, and she'd never had the chance to say good-bye.

All good, I can do this for her, I thought.

The woman began talking to me as if I were her dead father. She mentioned all the times she'd wanted a father who wasn't an alcoholic and who would just be her dad. She talked about her anger over his lying and not showing up at her school events and how he'd been disrespectful of her mom. She asked him why the alcohol meant more to him than being with her. *Don't you know you broke my heart?* she'd wept.

I lay there beneath the sheet, hearing the voices of my own daughters, as if they were speaking through her to me. I could feel all the feelings of a man who'd let an addiction come before all that was good and beautiful in his life. Beneath that sheet, I cried tears for my own babies, and I cried for the heartbreak of the woman sitting in that group room, reconciling her years of blaming herself for a dad who was lost in his own hell. Of course, his alcoholism was not her fault, just as my addiction was not my little girls' fault, but their hearts got broken anyway.

When we finished our process, I was asked to tell the woman how it felt to be her dad. What I shared with her was the truth of a man who could just as easily have been him, and every word was spoken with all the love and sorrow of someone who finally got it. On that particular day, that woman and I shared a gift of grace, a gift that touched both our souls and our family legacies. There was healing in those tears and a commitment to the truth and the freedom that was being offered from the experience.

✦ ✦ ✦

Psychodrama was just one of the processes we experienced in treatment. We also participated in a process called equine-assisted psychotherapy—big words for the magic of connecting horses and humans. We worked with horses in an amazing exploration of honesty in relationships. I had spent most of my life around horses, and the experience of connecting with them in treatment brought up a tidal wave of feelings and memories.

Horses are honest. They are not confused about what they are, nor are they interested in our stories about what we think we are. A horse knows the moment it looks at you if it trusts you or not. A horse doesn't confuse perception with rationalization. If the person working with the horse is genuine with their emotions, then the horse will trust them. If the person is disconnected and distorted in their emotions, the horse will be wary. Horses are survivors, they are flight animals, and they do not stay in a situation they don't trust.

In that regard they also look to the humans around them for leadership and confidence. When the human is a disconnected mess, the horse sees it and responds accordingly. The bottom line is, for all our masks and our proficiency at lying to ourselves, a horse isn't buying it. To be in treatment and realize that the animals are more honest than we are is very sobering. One day a week, we'd go to the corrals and spend an hour with the equine therapist and her beasts. I really struggled with the whole scene. The smells and sounds took me back through my whole life—from being a boy on my dad's ranch in Wyoming to being a man who worked horseback for a living.

I wanted to go home, and I wanted all this mess to just go away. That wasn't going to happen, so I had to show up and see where this opportunity could take me. The week before I left treatment, I was with my primary group when the therapist asked me to come into the center of the corral. As I did, she held her hands out and took mine and looked me straight in the eye.

"This isn't going to be an easy path for you, you know that," she said.

"Yes, I know it," I replied.

She kept on, "You're going to have to find a connection that's bigger than your addiction or you won't make it."

My heart was all in my throat. I also knew she was right.

"I want you to lie down here in the center of this corral and look up at the sky and let yourself go, just listen and see what's above you here and now."

As she walked away, I did what she'd asked and lay down on my back looking up. The sky was so blue and clouds so white. Then I heard the footsteps of the horses as they came toward me. I wasn't afraid. I knew a horse would never step on a person if it can possibly avoid it. Three of the horses moved slowly up to me and stood around, looking down at me as if they wanted me to know they were there. I could smell them. I could feel their breath. And everything went still for just a second, and, in that second, I felt total peace. This was where I belonged, with these guys, the horses. Horses had been with me all my life, and, like so many things that I loved, I had let them go for the insanity of living addicted.

When I got up, I looked at the therapist and said, "Thank you . . . I'm going to be okay, and I won't forget this. Thank you."

✦ ✦ ✦

We also participated in a "ropes" course. It was like an old military obstacle course that sets up participants to either ask for help—a huge step in itself—or find themselves stuck and unable to complete the challenge. Stuck was a very familiar feeling, and one that triggered the go-get-high demons.

Learning through metaphor was powerful; it allowed us to see the obvious without our defenses kicking in. When you're terrified of being honest, and honesty is the only way out of hell, it helps to have someone there who knows the tricks that allow us to reveal our truth. With every exercise and group experience, I learned more and more about myself and about the heart and minds that connect us all as humans. Moving from the depths of addiction and all those years of fear and loss to a place where I could almost believe that my life could change felt like a miracle. The realizations came in flashes, but then the awareness would fade away again. Like an exercise in choosing life over old beliefs and stories, I kept being brought into the moment to learn a lesson, but then my attention would drift back to the old thoughts and fears. The same was true for all of us.

We may not have wanted to see the truth, but accepting only what we wanted was what got us into this mess in the first place. The program was clever, in that we were allowed to discover for ourselves how we functioned as human beings. Every day was another "aha!" for me in how I came to be the guy who checked into this psych hospital.

What I began to realize was that my life was insane. It wasn't just me; it was the order of reality that I had accepted as fact. The world was insane; I was a product of that world. Most of my life was spent not being me. At the same time, the therapists were telling me that, ,if I wanted to change my behaviors, I couldn't continue to live the life I had created.

What the hell was I supposed to do? The thought of re-creating my life was suffocating. I couldn't breathe for fear of the idea of rearranging who I was. Most of my life had been spent fighting to get where I was. That it was out of control was secondary to my need to feel that this life was mine and that I could make it work.

At one point I met with my primary counselor in a one-on-one session, and he told me that the living arrangement I had created for myself was a setup for failure and that living in Tennessee, at the Ranch, and with my girlfriend in Florida did not give me the foundation I needed to keep myself accountable. I had a big reaction to this suggestion. *What the f—k does he know?* I wondered. I *had* to live like that. That's who I was, and I had business to take care of on both ends of that interstate.

What I was slow to recognize was this truth: I knew where to get dope from Vero Beach to Nashville. Every little town and hotel along the way was an opportunity to stop over and get loaded without anyone but me knowing. I didn't want to do that anymore. Just the memory of being up all night with some local party queen along with the sick guilty feeling and dreading the all-day drive to get where I was supposed to be was a nightmare.

If I couldn't be who I thought I was, then who was I? The fear triggered cravings to get high. How perfect that I was in a treatment center! I was determined to deal with my addiction. But I was not interested in re-creating who I was. It didn't occur to me that I couldn't change the most powerful relationship in my life without changing all of it. I wanted a divorce from my Peruvian princess—while everything else stayed the same.

✦ ✦ ✦

The primary focus in treatment was the diagnosis. Whether that diagnosis was focused on an aspect of our personality or an addiction, the attention was on the symptoms and behaviors that got us there. As the days went by, we were made more aware of the underlying disease that fed our issues, and the primary attention was still on our diagnosis. That made it easier for me to believe that all I needed to do was stop acting out in my addiction and my life would be okay. In my mind, I could reason that the problem was cocaine and my affinity for the high. I used that belief to keep the rest of my life off-limits from close examination. In the same sentence, I could defend my drug use because I wasn't happy with my life and then refuse to unravel my life because my problem was only using drugs. Like I said, I was crazy.

As I shared what was happening with me, the counselors guided me toward an awareness of my reactions. The lesson was powerful and frightening. If I weren't careful, I'd be out the door, off to see the Wizard of Hell. I really didn't want to do that. Lost means lost, not knowing where you are, no recognition of your surroundings. I hung above the abyss with no bottom in sight. That darkness was too terrifying to look into. What was happening to me? I had come to treatment to learn to address my addiction to cocaine, and now I was losing hold of who I was.

Initially, I thought changing my behaviors would fix my life. I had it backward; the truth was that addressing my life would fix my behaviors. I was out of control because my life was not authentic. My behaviors were symptoms of a lack of true fulfillment. I clung to my identities as a rancher, musician, and commodities trader, because that was all I had. All I knew myself to be was what I did. Of course it was terrifying to hear that everything had to change.

They also said that, to recover, I had to quit using any kind of mind-altering substances. Nothing, *nada*—not a beer, not a glass of wine, not even a hit on a joint. If I wanted to recover, I had to quit everything—even sex. That's right. They told me that I should not get into a relationship for at least six months. That sure sounded and felt drastic. *Holy shit! What have I done?* Suddenly the entire dynamic of what I was doing in treatment took on an ominous reality. *Damn, man, just how sick am I?*

✦ ✦ ✦

Throughout treatment, I did my best to be honest. The therapists constantly challenged my thoughts and perceptions. They said I couldn't trust my own thinking. There's an old 12-Step saying that we were supposed to take to heart: "My best thinking got me here."

My life was a mess, but it was the result of my doing the best I could with the hand I was dealt. I didn't feel like my life was over, just lost. The intense fear and judgment of the treatment process was a powerful contradiction to the "happy, joyous, and free" that I wanted. What I was missing was an awareness of how life could become such a mess.

Drug and alcohol treatment is based in the philosophy and examples in *The Big Book of Alcoholics Anonymous*. The program I had admitted myself to had grown out of that foundation. There was a clear presentation that we suffer from the beliefs and experiences of our lives and from the symptoms of our diagnosis. When you're a drug addict, you do ridiculous amounts of drugs in an attempt to deal with the misery of being you. Bulimics puke, alcoholics drink, sex addicts have sex, and so on. The behaviors of those in treatment are in truth the symptoms of a life of suffering. When you're not comfortable in your own skin, medicating is not an unreasonable response. In America today, we are brainwashed to believe that more is the answer to everything. Our lives were a mess because we were alcoholics and addicts, and we were alcoholics and addicts because our lives were a mess.

The foundation assumption was that our society, and humanity as a whole, was good, and, if we would just behave and fit in, then we would be okay. That assumption was a lie. Humanity is ruled by fear, and what I suffered from was a disconnection from myself that fitting into society was not going to correct. I found myself torn between wanting to believe what I was told and feeling that something was very incongruent about the process. I had a lot of questions of the counselors that were met with arrogant responses. The counselors seemed to have black-and-white points of view on the recovery process. They tried to convince me they were right. After all, they had years of experience, and they were invested in their beliefs. I wanted to believe in "happy, joyous, and free." Without that, what was the point? If what I was dealing with was an incurable disease, then how was I supposed to ever achieve "happy, joyous, and free?"

In recovery we have the power to choose to reframe our relationship with life itself, which offers the opportunity to completely re-create who we are. "Happy, joyous, and free" didn't resonate with terminal disease or keeping score by counting clean days. Sure, I was proud of the days that went by that I hadn't used, but I was not going to attach my sense of self-worth to that number of days. Not using kept me from hurting myself with that particular behavior, the behavior of an addict, but not using was not a source of fulfillment. Fulfillment is the result of what we do for ourselves, not what we don't do.

Not acting out in our addictions can be perceived as an act of self-love or as the choice to not indulge in a behavior out of fear. Loving myself is fulfilling, while not indulging out of fear is an act of resistance, a battle of will over obsession. They are different points of view of the same situation, offering very different perceptions of us. I was tired of doing battle with myself. Believing that all I was was an addict fed the struggle. To believe that I was a human being dealing with an addiction offered me the experience of caring for myself, which for me was a new concept.

Those contradictions fed my tendency to do everything my way. I had to choose to either accept what I was told and be a member of the recovery club, or do things my way and be an outcast. For all the blessings and miracles that recovery offered, I could not resist doing battle over the contradictions in the process.

Among my labels I had been tagged an alcoholic and a codependent. They did not fit. Codependency means you are willing to sacrifice yourself for the sake of being in relationship with others. I was the opposite of that. If you didn't like the way I did things, you could leave any time. The argument for my being an alcoholic was that "all coke addicts must be alcoholic." There were studies that backed this opinion. As lost as I was, I knew what an addiction was and that was my relationship with cocaine. Alcohol was a medicator in my life, not an addiction. Now the point was not whether I agreed not to indulge in drugs or alcohol of any type; that commitment to myself made sense. My resistance was to the professionals' investment in deciding what was true for me regardless of how I felt about it.

✦ ✦ ✦

The 12-Step fellowship was created by a divine inspiration. Bill W. channeled the steps like a mystic channels the word of God. Being a fellowship, the program was built around "suggestions" and traditions, and, in fact, the Big Book says, "We can recover." As powerful and effective as the steps can be, they are not the Holy Grail. They are a tool, one of many, many tools that support healing and reconnection.

There are some basic conflicts in using the 12-Step program as a professional treatment model. In fact, the program states that it should remain nonprofessional. Alcoholics Anonymous places a high value on each person's discovering that he or she is addicted. Recovery is offered only by way of suggestions. The group or sponsor doesn't have an investment in anyone's believing what they say. They care, of course, but they talk out of their own experience and leave it for you to decide what works for you. Twelve-Step philosophy doesn't believe in money for services rendered. It is to be offered purely on a spiritual level. That helps keep ego out of it. Twelve-Steppers work the steps at their own speed—allowing Spirit to guide the process. Treatment centers have an investment in their clients' believing in what they say. They work on a time schedule that, for the most part, is guided by insurance companies. These are minor differences, and they are huge.

The counselors at the center all meant well, and they were talented in their work. Plus they were only following orders from the higher-ups. But there is wisdom in the 12-Step program that doesn't translate into treatment. The energy of the 12-Step fellowship was not intended to be a book of rules used to control addicts; it was not intended to be used as a basis of judgment for how compliant a patient in treatment is or how "much they want it" (*it* being recovery). It seemed like a misuse of a beautiful practice to turn spiritual inspiration into business models. The corrupted version (if only slightly corrupted) triggered my resentment, and I would end up paying a big price for it.

Once again the issue became whether or not I would accept and do what I was told versus being supported in figuring myself out for myself. If all the addicts and alcoholics in the world could just accept being told what to do in order to be okay, we wouldn't need treatment programs; we'd just need an instruction book.

From the moment my recovery journey began, I was done with accepting what was, just because the majority had come to agreement on it. I was not interested in taking refuge in another belief system. Like Waylon Jennings said, "This is the big time. There are no dress rehearsals. We are professionals."

I decided to take responsibility for myself, and all that comes with it.

CHAPTER 8

On Thin Ice

When I left the treatment center, I felt like I had been set free behind enemy lines. I knew the territory, but I didn't trust anyone. I had been in the bubble of the treatment center's compound for six weeks—six weeks of deep emotional, spiritual, and physical soul searching. My emotional body had been blown wide open, and now I had to go back into the jungle and survive. Against the therapist's strongest advice, I decided to spend a couple of days in Tucson with a woman I'd met in treatment. She was a sweetheart whose life experiences had offered her more than her fair share of nightmares. We were going to journey around southern Arizona to do some sightseeing. It seemed innocent enough. Three days later, she overdosed on crack and almost died.

The loneliness faced by people in treatment and early recovery can feel overwhelming. Our daily survival had been propped up by our relationship with our medicators. In treatment, we were given the lowdown on what those medicators had done to our lives. The space that's created when we allow that truth to sink in can feel like a deep empty hole, one that could swallow us at any moment. So there is a natural longing to find someone or something to cling to, to keep from feeling that loneliness. It had been easy for us to leave treatment together. Neither of us wanted to be alone, and going straight home didn't feel right.

I thought I had it all figured out. We would stay in a cool old inn in downtown Tucson, go see the sights around southern Arizona for a couple of days, and then head home reacclimated to life on the outside. After checking in, we looked at each other. We had one room, but we were not supposed to sleep together. Okay, fine. And we could not get loaded. That was okay, too. As the sun began to set, we walked to the dining room, feeling as if we had it all together. We were in agreement that we would respect the suggestions of our therapists—except, of course, the one that we not stay together. That first night was great. We had supper, watched a movie, and crashed early.

The next day we took off for Tombstone and a tour of the area. It was springtime in southern Arizona and beautiful. Everything seemed perfect. We got back to the inn late that afternoon and went to the bar. Neither of us saw ourselves as having an issue with alcohol, so we got a couple of margaritas. Two drinks later, we were talking about finding some coke. It didn't take long to score. We were both professionals at finding our way around the wrong part of town. As soon as we got back to the hotel, we got high and naked.

Over the next forty-eight hours, we went through a couple thousand dollars of coke. On the second morning, she left in a taxi to pick up some more. When she got back, I knew something wasn't right. When I questioned her, she told me she'd gotten too high in the cab on the way back and had passed out.

I told her, "You don't need to smoke any more coke."

She said, "I know. I better take a break."

By this time we were both regretting what we were doing, but there was still coke left. So we turned on the TV and tried to watch a movie. She got up and headed off to the bathroom. When she came out a few minutes later, a big cloud of crack smoke followed her. Halfway to the bed, she went into a seizure. I prayed to God she wouldn't die there like that. As I held her, I called the front desk and told them to call an ambulance. By the time the ambulance crew got there, she was semiconscious again. She didn't know where she was or how she got there. The paramedic asked me what had happened. I told him I didn't know.

He looked at me and said, "Look, man, she's obviously OD'ed. We don't call the law; it's against policy. If we did no one would call us when this happens. So we need to know what's happened with her."

I told him the whole story. They took her to an ER, and I picked her up a couple of hours later. We went from heaven to hell and barely survived the fall. I knew that day what we were facing was for keeps. There was not always going to be another chance. I've never been more terrified.

The next day, we packed up and headed home. She went back to the hell she'd left behind in New Orleans, and I flew back to the Ranch in Tennessee. We talked a few times after that, but I never saw her again. I sometimes wonder how she's doing and hope she's well.

❖ ❖ ❖

Walking back into the world was a bittersweet experience. After the nightmare in Tucson, I knew I was on thin ice. I went back and forth between using and staying clean for the first year following treatment. The challenge was to reconnect with the life I'd left behind and redefine all of the relationships that made it up. I expected the world to recognize the changes in me and respond accordingly. That was a joke. After twenty years of being the life of the party, it was not realistic to believe that the people I'd run with for years would realize and respect that I was trying to change my life.

Every time my phone rang, I worried who might be on the other end. I had several old party friends who were ready to come over with dope and hang out all night. It was difficult enough dealing with my own cravings, much less trying to deal with friends putting that temptation in my face. I did what I believed was my best, but, when there was a good-looking woman with a bag of dope wanting to come in and play—well, like they say in the rooms of AA, "It's progress, not perfection."

At this point, I began to see how important it was for me to find a solid support system if I really wanted to let go of my addiction. Despite my reluctance to blindly accept their belief system, a 12-Step program was my most obvious choice for support. Personal importance was my greatest obstacle. I recognized my addiction to cocaine, but what I didn't agree with was the belief that, if I used any mind-altering substance at all, I was going to end up as bad off as if I'd gone straight to my drug of choice. That just did not make sense to me. The 12-Step programs were black-and-white on that issue. I was still having an occasional beer or glass of wine, and that seemed to be okay with me. So if I were to go to AA, I couldn't talk about my version of the program or I'd risk being attacked like a Hasid in Mecca. I was cocky, not stupid. The same rules applied at Narcotics Anonymous.

It took almost two months after I left treatment to get to my first meeting. After Tucson, I was afraid of getting high again. Fear alone, though, was not enough to keep me from the dark side. The difference in me following treatment was that I could no longer pretend it was all right—even when I was high. Reclaiming my sobriety and will was a double-edged sword. My ego believed I could manage my situation if I would just be smart about where and what I did. On the other hand, my heart was broken into a million little pieces over the reality of all that I had dealt with in treatment. I didn't want to be sick anymore. I knew that what I had been doing was in total disrespect of life. I wanted to change, but I didn't know how. Being me was hell, but I was not going to give it up.

Awareness has a mystical power. It stays in your mind, wanted or not, reminding you of what you know to be true. I finally got more disgusted with the drugging than I was resistant to 12-Step programs.

CHAPTER 9

Meeting at 202

My first meeting outside treatment was at the 202 Club in West Nashville. I knew the neighborhood. I had partied there for years. The Gold Rush and the Exit/Inn were gathering places of the late-'70s music scene in Nashville. That was a lot of miles ago. It was now June 1997. I hadn't been to a meeting since leaving treatment, and I needed one. The parking lot was almost full. *Damn*, I thought, *there are a lot of people in there.*

So I sat and listened to Steve Earle singing the song he wrote for the late great Townes Van Zandt. Townes drank himself to death, living what should only be imagined. That's the downside of a go-to-hell attitude; if you're not careful, you will. That's why I was there. I didn't want that anymore, and I didn't have much faith that I could avoid it. I had lived most of my adult life being what I did. From musician and cowboy to commodities trader, whatever my gig was, I was. Since treatment, I had realized maybe I wasn't what I did. Maybe

I was something else. Whatever that something else was would have to wait a little longer. I needed to get through that door and into the AA meeting inside. I was scared. I was self-conscious. I felt alone.

As Earle's "Fort Worth Blues" ended, I climbed out of my pickup and walked into the back door of the 202 Club. The house was full of people, but, contrary to my fear, nobody stopped or even paid any attention to my being there. I immediately felt safe. I wasn't alone anymore. That's what I needed—safety, somewhere to go when the noise in my head was out of control, which was most of the time. That alone was terrifying, like sitting on a surfboard a hundred yards offshore and having a ten-foot shark swim by.

When it's just you and life and death, you realize real quick how much faith you don't have. My craving to get high was that shark, and he had been circling for two days. I couldn't white-knuckle it anymore. So here I was, I had made it to 202. Looking around, the scene resembled a clubhouse, people hanging out, talking and laughing. The meeting was upstairs. Climbing the stairs, I heard someone reading from *The Big Book.*

Turning the corner on the second floor, I walked into a room full of all shapes, sizes, and colors of human beings—a tribe of survivors. There was a thick blue cloud of cigarette smoke hanging over the gathering. I sat against an outside wall as the meeting opened. *Thank you, God, I can breathe again.* I felt like I had just held my breath for the whole hour's drive to Nashville. An hour earlier, I could have just as easily gone to see the dope dealer. I was so sure and afraid that was where I was headed that turning left on to the road leading to 202 seemed like a miracle.

I was only a few blocks away from the cocaine queen of Music Row. Those memories of her gave me a sick butterflies-in-the-stomach feeling. This time I had made another choice; those butterflies were gone, and I was so grateful to be sitting in this roomful of others who were walking through their own valley of the shadow. We weren't alone; we had each other.

Sitting and listening, I flashed back to my time in treatment when my counselor told me that getting high would never really be okay with me again. After the opening readings, the chairperson opened the floor for a topic. The guy sitting next to me spoke softly, "My name's Lonely, and I'm an addict and alcoholic."

He started talking about the last few months of his life and how he had gone back to drugging after a couple of years clean. This was his first meeting since he had quit using, and he was tired, scared, and fed up with how narrow his choices seemed. I was overwhelmed by the feeling that he was talking to me.

Once again, I flashed back on memories of treatment and how sweet the bond had been among all of us who shared that space together. This was that same feeling revisited—alive and well right here at 202. As I looked around the room, I saw compassion and understanding. *Thank you, Father. I am so grateful. I don't want to be alone anymore.* I wasn't.

I didn't speak at that meeting. As the conversation moved around the room, the stories were of similar experiences shared by people who had never officially met but had all taken refuge in the same hell, one that seemed the only way out. I thought to myself, *Thank you, buddy. Thank you for making it here.*

I didn't need to know anything to feel gratitude for the safety of sitting in that meeting at 202. The experience was the truth. That's all I needed to know. After the meeting, I hung out and talked to a couple of guys about the struggle of changing years of addiction. "Keep coming back." That's the cliché as well as the truth.

Walking outside I was hit by the heavy humid heat of a June night in Nashville—90 degrees and 90 percent humidity. I realized I hadn't even been conscious of the heat when I first arrived. That's the power of obsession. It's amazing how lost we can become, and it's even more amazing that we can make our way back. We do the first because that's the world we are born into. We do the second because we are not of this world. We are that spirit that won't be trapped by definition. We are that light that acts for us when the shadows would have us believe only lies.

With the insanity of this world, it is no wonder that we trust so little and fear so much. That's who I was: one who really trusted very little and feared most of all. From that point of view, all the obsessions, addictions, guilt, shame, and fear made sense. I was the product of a world and a culture that had chosen knowledge over life and opinions over truth. That is who I *had been*, and I was realizing that was not who I had to be. I could choose again.

Making that first meeting at 202 was the second phase of a path of first experiences. The first phase had been checking myself into the treatment center. Going to that meeting at 202 had shown me that knowing what I was doing was nowhere near as important as just showing up and letting life show me. To this day, I still feel the relief of making that first meeting. That old house had seen a lot of hard living and had heard a lot of tough stories. It felt to me like what a church ought to feel like if the people inside would only get as honest.

While my answer to the question of "Could I drink a beer without getting drunk or moving on to my drug of choice?" was yes, I believed I could, the more significant question was, "Is playing with fire worth the risk?" And, could I accept the guidance of those who had walked their own path of recovery and not have to learn everything the hard way? This last question revealed a truth about my relationship with myself. Being right was more important to me than accepting or being accepted. It didn't matter what was in my best interest; I was determined to be right, as if right were the bearer of happiness.

Even in my relationships, I would push the envelope by dating women who liked to get high. The plan was to be honest about my situation and as responsible as I could short of staying away from that type of person. It's amazing to me how insidious the drug conscience can be. One woman I dated for a few months was completely support-ive of my staying away from cocaine until one of her friends gave her some, and, well, she thought we might do just a little together. Hell, she was crazier on it than I was. I ended up leaving her house at five in the morning when she left to go get more. I didn't date her again.

For most of my life I had not acknowledged the consequences of my choices. I either ignored them or pretended they never happened. In my twisted mind, I equated personal responsibility with being judged. When we believe we're not good enough, responsibility is usually about what we've done wrong. On top of that, not having faith in ourselves is a setup for constant self-judgment. We create our reality by projecting our beliefs and feelings out onto the world around us. What was most familiar in my world was me being the one who could have or should have done better. At some point, I realized that I would sabotage myself because letting myself down was what I expected myself to do.

All of this insanity went around in my head while I tried to stay away from white powder. I got more involved in AA and NA. I needed the safety and community of the 12-Step programs. The obsessive nature of addiction puts incredible pressure on you. That pressure makes the refuge of your old familiar hell seem inviting. In those moments, the program can be all that lies between you and doing it again.

I didn't have to agree with everything to get what I needed in the moment. The answer lay in my willingness to accept help. I wasn't through trying to figure things out, but I could see that I needed some help. My shell of personal importance finally cracked. Maybe

I didn't have all the answers. Maybe I could stand to learn a thing or two about life.

I settled in at home in Tennessee. I had to create a relationship with the process of recovery to help keep me grounded. The transition from treatment to the outside world was rough. Then one of those miracles happened. You know, one of those miracles that happen when you're in a place where you can recognize them?

CHAPTER 10

A Deeper Level of Determination

The phone rang.

"Hey, Cowboy, how's it going?"

It was Sandy—the counselor who had done my intake interview when I checked into the treatment center.

"I'm getting by," I replied truthfully. "I'm actually going to meetings now. I guess I've decided I can't do this alone. So what's up with you? It's good to hear your voice."

"I'm glad you're not trying to do it alone. You don't have to," she said, her voice sounding upbeat. "Anyway there's a company that used to be connected to our treatment center that holds recovery workshops. They do amazing work, and I just heard they are moving to Cumberland Furnace. That's close to you, right?"

"Yeah, very close," I replied.

"They're looking for an equine contractor. They do four-day equine-assisted psychotherapy workshops. If you're interested, I can get you their phone number. It would be good for you to stay connected to that process. You could learn a lot from them."

Instant relief washed over me, like God had sent me an angel. In fact, God had, and I knew it. I had forty horses on the ranch, and ten or twelve of them were as smart and easygoing as they get. As our conversation moved on to life in Nashville and who was up to what around the music scene, I got nervous about not being good enough to work with this new opportunity. "You know, Sandy, I haven't won any awards for buying into the recovery world's point of view," I told her.

She shooed away my concerns. "Don't worry about that. You just keep doing your best. I think you'd be a great connection for them. Just make the phone call and leave the rest up to Spirit."

I made the call and left the rest up to Spirit just as she suggested. The new situation became a true blessing in my life. The director came out to see my setup, and everything came together. Two months later, I was working my first four-day program. The opportunity and responsibility of working the equine programs really helped ground me. I got a taste of the gift of giving back and being there for others in a soul sense.

Equine-assisted psychotherapy is pure magic. Horses are perfect mirrors for humans. They see through us. A horse trusts what they see and feel. You can't bullshit them. In the workshops, each participant chose a horse to work with for the three days of the program. What the participants don't realize is that not only do the horses mirror the internal state of the participant, the therapist can see how that person moves in relationship to life just by the way he or she moves around the horses.

To be a good equine therapist is an artistic gift; some people have it, and some don't. I had lived with animals all my life and had no

idea how much awareness I had of the human/horse connection.
From the earliest workshops, I could see what the therapists were
seeing. In fact, I caught subtleties they would sometimes miss. The
experience was magic.

We connect to the truth in healing. There is a peace in the place
where time stands still. We bridge the gap between the moment in
healing and those who passed the wounds of humanity on to us.
It's not personal. Healing is really restoring the truth in place of
an inheritance of lies. Truth is timeless. When we touch truth, we
touch the infinite. In those equine programs, we touched the truth
every day. Some people were able to let go of their suffering; some
weren't. They all did their best, and they were all a blessing to me and
to my own progress. I saw myself in the lives and stories of all who
participated. I realized how resistant I was to change, how accepting
I was of fear, and how afraid I was that I would always be lonely. I
also found a deeper level of determination to undo everything that
stood between who I believed I was and freedom. Life had begun to
very slowly reorganize itself.

When I left for treatment, I had been involved in two lawsuits.
My dad used to say there are a lot of things people will do for money
that aren't worth it. When you grow up with money, you realize how
much it is not the cure-all some believe it is. Looking outside one's
self for fulfillment is one of the great shell games in life—money or
no money. It is also the domain of the great liar, the one that tells us
we are not good enough and that the trinkets of this world can solve
our problems. The world we live in is the result of our problem, not
the answer to it.

My legal situations were finally resolved to no one's satisfaction,
except that they were done. I let go of South Florida and moved back
to Tennessee full time.

✦ ✦ ✦

Working as an equine contractor became the highlight of my life. We did five events a year. From spring to fall, I connected to grace through those workshops. To be close to people sharing their deepest and darkest secrets brings an appreciation of all that it means to be human. When people come together to heal themselves, miracles happen.

One program included a nineteen-year-old girl. She had been using drugs and alcohol since the age of twelve and had been sober for a year or so. As her story unraveled, she talked about her dad and how he had always been an alcoholic until he died from the physical complications of his alcoholism. Of course she got high; she'd been raised to get high. To her credit, she also saw the self-imposed suffering that addiction brought. She knew she was doing it to herself, and she wanted out. The catch for her, like it was for so many, was that she suffered at the deepest level from a broken heart.

The drugs and alcohol had been the way she was taught to deal with the pain of life. Bullshit is so pervasive in our society and hypocrisy such a standard that we're actually taught by example to hurt ourselves when we're hurting and to blame ourselves for what's not working. This is all so that we can judge ourselves as wrong with all the self-righteous support of our family and friends, leaving us alone to do more of the same over and over.

That little girl's heart had been broken, and there had been no one there to tell her that a broken heart was what she really suffered from. The addictions were symptoms of that heartbreak, not the cause. On the third day of the equine program, she talked about her dad and how she missed the love she could have had from him. As the group sat in a circle, the therapist asked if she'd be willing to choose someone to play her dad in a psychodrama.

My heart jumped as she looked me in the eye and asked if I would
be her dad.

"Of course I will," I replied with a lump in my throat.

Paulette, the therapist, asked her to talk to me and tell me how she
felt about her experiences growing up, prompting to be completely
honest. As I listened, I felt the love, the longing, the anger, and the
sadness of what this girl had lived. I felt the regret and pain of knowing what it's like to be a father out of control and lost in the misery
of an addiction.

When she was through talking, I looked her in the eye, and, in
my role as her father, I told her what I knew as a father myself, how
sorry I was, and how there was no excuse for the loss she had suffered. I told her I loved her and that, if I could, I'd take back all the
pain I'd ever caused in her life, but I couldn't do that. What was done
was done. I told her the truth as I knew it to be, and, as I spoke, she
seemed to let go of some of the anger and self-judgment she had
taken on over the years.

You see, when the people we love don't love us back, we usually
blame ourselves as not being good enough. We think it's our fault.
Looking her straight in the eye, I told her how proud I was that she
had the courage and strength to find a better way to work through her
heartbreak. I told her how proud I was that she had broken the cycle
of alcohol and drugs that had been the choice of so many generations
of our family before her. I told her I loved her no matter what, and I
meant it. I meant it in the role as her dad and as myself.

Sitting there in that circle of people, we shared the truth of who
we really were, and that is the truth that will set us free from all that
would keep us bound to the legacy of fear and suffering that has
become the foundation of life in this world.

What happened there that day was a recurring experience in those
workshops. What we shared wasn't magic; it was grace and truth from

two people who had met just days before, through our willingness to step beyond what we thought we knew and who we believed we were. The truth of the unconditional love that is life helped us to begin to resolve what we had both, in our own way, lived as the inheritance of being human. We would not settle for that old lie anymore.

✦ ✦ ✦

On another occasion I worked with a man my age who, by all accounts, should have been dead from numerous overdoses. He had done a lot of personal healing work, and he was still stuck on a poisonous resentment toward his brother. For two days he worked around how his suffering had been perpetrated by his brother's being the favorite in his family. By the third day, he'd realized that he was the one hurting himself with his resentment. The challenge was that his story was so old and ingrained that the anger kept flashing back, and his reaction to that anger was automatic. In vain, he had done his best to forgive his brother, but that forgiveness had been from the point of view that his brother was still responsible for his suffering, but he'd forgive him anyway. His forgiveness was conditional and based in judgment of his brother.

I asked him if he'd be willing to get on the horse and have the horse represent his relationship with his brother. He replied, "Sure, whatever you think."

I told him, "No, that's not it. This is not about what anyone else thinks. This is about what you believe and how you see yourself in this relationship with your brother. This really has nothing to do with your brother."

Anger flashed across his face, and I looked him in the eye and said, "Do you trust you?"

He stopped and looked at the ground. "No, I don't really trust me."

"Do you trust your anger?"

"I hate my anger."

"Do you trust this process?"

"I'm trying to."

"Okay, are you willing to see this horse as your relationship with your brother?"

"Yes."

"Do you feel the difference between that *Yes* and *Sure, whatever you think*?"

"Yes, I do; let's do it."

We put him on the horse, but not on his butt. We put him over the horse on his belly, like a dead man in the old cowboy movies. When I asked him how he felt, he said it felt familiar. It was hard to breathe, and it was familiar. *Bingo!* As I led the horse around, I asked him, "Who is in charge of this relationship? Can you see where you're going?"

Then he said, "Stop, this is bullshit. I've been doing this my whole life."

"Doing what?"

"Being led around like my brother was responsible for me."

"Is he responsible for you?"

"No, he is not."

"What would you like to do?"

Just as I asked the question, the horse bucked up a little and the client slid off, landing on his feet. We were all momentarily stunned by how perfect that had been. I asked the client if he was all right, and he started laughing.

The horse turned and put his head on the client's chest, completely still. Then the tears came, sadness, gratitude, love, letting go. We were in a corral on a ranch in Tennessee, and everyone there felt the presence of what we really are when we stop trying so hard to be what we think we are.

Looking at the client, I said, "I've got one more thing to ask of you."

"Sure."

"It's a mantra for you. 'I will no longer accept my excuses for suffering.'"

He repeated, "I will no longer accept my excuses for my suffering."

I added, "I am responsible for my life."

"I am responsible for my life," he repeated.

That was several years ago, and I occasionally see that man around. He always smiles and repeats that mantra. Life works when we stop holding it hostage.

✦ ✦ ✦

The book *A Course in Miracles* by the Foundation for Inner Peace says that miracles are naturally occurring events. What is not natural is how we stand in their way. In our fear and desperation, we create misery in place of faith. The Bible quotes Yeshua saying, "When two or more gather in my name, I will be there." He did not mean him, the man. He meant Him, the Spirit, the Christ energy. This is *not* about any religion. Jesus—who is called Christ—was a Rabbi who has been quoted as saying, " I am the Light of the World" and "The Kingdom of Heaven is within you and all around you, and men do not have the eyes to see it."

This energy, this light, far exceeds the very limited nature of our belief systems and the stories we tell. This light is a part of all of us. When we come together in love and support of one another, that light shines. That light is the truth of what we are. The life you're leaving behind has a will of its own; it will do all it can to keep you in its grasp. Your freedom means a little piece of hell is transformed into light. As blind and out of control as I was, I was making my way back into the light.

My work with the equine programs continued for three years, until the program was relocated to new property. I cannot express the power of the gifts I received during that time. To be present as people work through the experiences in their lives that have come to haunt them is to realize how connected we truly are. At some point I realized that what I was witnessing in the work I was doing was the transformation of the legacies of the clients' families. What we suffer from will be addressed and transformed or passed on.

The legacy of humanity has been one of suffering and fear. I call it the "I-am-not." I am not good enough or rich enough or smart enough or whatever enough. The core belief underlying the foundation of suffering in this world is that we are less than we should be; that no matter how much we do, we'll always fall short of what we could have been if only we had tried harder. The *I-am-not* will always include a criticism or judgment that, if indulged, will prevent us from simply appreciating the moment.

Healing the legacies of our families and our races brings the *I-am-not* face to face with the truth. The truth is that we are everything we are created to be, and more. In the equine programs I saw the truth. I saw the transformation and the love of one person expressed by being there for another in strength and truth. With the horses as our mediators, the clients found the answers they had been looking for, the answers that no one else could give them. The truth is the truth and has always been within each of us. We've just never been taught how to listen, or, more important, how to trust.

Working with the horses holds up an amazing mirror. I've learned more about how to deal with relationships working with horses than I learned in forty years of watching people. A horse is always a horse. They are never confused about who or what they are. They give what they get, plain and simple.

During my time in treatment, I went through the same equine process I later assisted in at home. Being so close to the horses made me realize how much of a gift they are in my life. I love them and everything about them, including the smell and feel of them. Through their honesty, they brought me closer to my own.

CHAPTER 11

Accepting Responsibility

Sharing my love of the horses with the people who attended the equine programs heightened my awareness. I was learning how to feel again. Living took on a new light. As each person worked through their experiences and feelings, the whole group connected to the flow. I was living in a special place.

Time after time, someone commented on the magic of the land. As the pieces came together in my mind, I saw a vision of what could be. Life was guiding me, and I was finally in a place where I could feel and acknowledge that guidance. It was time for me to bring my vision into the light.

Middle Tennessee is a magical place. Before the Europeans arrived, middle Tennessee was a shared hunting and fishing ground. The native people knew that humans could not own the land. We are the caretakers and beneficiaries of the land. In the summer, the hills of middle Tennessee are so green and alive that you can taste it in the air. In the early morning a mist rises from the river and out of the hollows that seems to highlight the shroud between this world and the next. In autumn, the leaves fall to the ground, a blanket of color, leaving the open spaces between the trees clear so that we might see it as new. Beauty reveals itself everywhere.

From the singing of the birds to the smell of the wood smoke and the warmth of the fireplaces, life seems simpler there. At Pinewood Farm, one of our ranches, an Italian marble statue that John Graham, the founder of the farm, had shipped from Italy stands vigil over his family cemetery.

Graham bought the home tract of the property from a black man named Davis. That was before the Civil War when white men didn't have to pay black men for property. He did anyway. (Coincidently, I bought the property for a white man named Davis, A.D., my stepdad.) Graham and his brother built a 5,000-acre plantation and never owned a slave. In fact, the story goes that he bought a slave once only to give the man his freedom and some money to travel on. During the late 1800s Pinewood Farm was a very prosperous place that never took sides in the "War Between the States." Graham also never allowed alcohol on his property—not because he was against it, but because he would not tolerate the hangovers and chaos that came with it. His people had work to do, and that was that.

During the Civil War, Pinewood Farm sold hemp rope and other supplies to both sides, which kept the Union army from burning him out. There are 5,000-year-old arrowheads and spear points that still come to the surface all over the place following heavy rains and plowing of the ground. For everyone from the native people and John Graham to A.D. Davis and my mom, and now me, that land has always been a place of vision.

As I was waking up to my truth as a human being, I began to see everything in a different light. If I told you that the land showed me what I was to do with it, I would not be telling tales. It didn't tell me in words; it told me in love and in the experience of working those equine programs. I knew I was supposed to do something. I knew those ranches were about more than just running cows. Then I got it.

The ranches I lived on offered a perfect setting for a residential healing/treatment program. I wouldn't be short on staff, as I was connected to a group of incredibly gifted therapists with years of experience in the treatment field. As I began to share my vision with some people in the recovery community, I found support for the idea. My dream of what would become the Ranch was born.

About this time, my youngest daughter, Ana, decided she wanted to live with me. She loved being with me and on the ranches. Maybe it's in our blood, but she found her heart's connection with the horses and cattle. Both of my daughters loved the ranch life, and both are great horse people. However, the older of the two, Alexis, was more attached to her mom, and rightfully so—I had spent years missing in action. Despite that, Ana was still her daddy's girl, and that was a saving grace for me.

My love for my girls is the sweetest gift I have ever known, and separation from them had been painful. To have my daughter come home gave me a home again. Waking up in the morning with a good feeling about the day, fixing breakfast for my little girl, and then driving her to school was a gift from the angels. I got to be her dad without all the drama of my relationship with her mom. For the first time in her life, I was dependable. There were plenty of struggles and a lot of challenges, but I was with my baby, and nothing was more important than that. I had shifted my relationship to the addiction. There was still energy there along with the pull from time to time, but I had found a way to be more grounded. I had done so much work on myself and let so much of the old heavy energy of guilt and shame go that I could follow through on my decision to say no. I was regaining my self-respect, and my heart was back in the center of my being rather than being buried under all the sadness and craziness.

My process kept moving forward: I attended 12-Step meetings several times a week along with my weekly therapy group and the equine programs. There was something in each day that kept me present and focused. There were people I had known for years without ever really knowing them who became my guardian angels. Two of my most supportive friends were a couple of the most talented songwriters in Nashville. We had spent time riding horseback together. They enjoyed helping move the cows from pasture to pasture. When I got home from treatment, they called to tell me they loved me and would be there for me anytime I needed support.

I started going to *A Course in Miracles* class with one of them, and we became even closer than before. She was gay, so I knew our relationship wasn't going anywhere physically, but I had to ask anyway—you know, that "cowboy charm" thing. She wasn't having it. Still, as my heart opened, the universe responded with all the love and light that I could handle. I fell completely in love with my lesbian friend and learned for the first time in my life that sex does not define love. Sex is an expression of love and only one of an infinite number of ways to express it.

Living was still a roller coaster, but the ride didn't hit nearly as many high highs or low lows. The challenges of being in the cattle business, trading commodities, and creating the Ranch kept me moving. I was driven to succeed, to follow through on the plans and dreams I had shared with my dad and A.D. My relationship with the cattle business was an extension of my relationships with them. That was the one family legacy I wanted to stay attached to.

Attachments serve to keep me connected to people and situations. Those connections hold a lot of energy, my energy. A major part of my recovery process was to examine all my relationships and attachments. I had a lot of powerful attachments that no longer served me. To change those attachments, I had to break the agreements I had with myself. One real obvious one was the resentment I felt toward my ex-wife. I was big-time attached to that resentment, and it served only to make me miserable. We were done, so what was the point? Making her wrong was not going to make my life better.

My victim attitude demanded that I judge her. That is insanity. I was giving up time and space in my life to be hateful toward someone I didn't want anything else to do with. It was time to learn how to let go of years of guilt, shame, judgment, and emotional poison. We even tried seeing each other a few times, going out with friends to clubs and parties. I was so stuck on not knowing how to let go that I came full circle and tried to figure out if we could work again. I was beginning to realize that sobriety and sanity may not have as much in common as I had assumed. We were not going to get back together. It didn't take long to realize I had been punishing myself for having believed I was not good enough for her.

Not all attachments were as loaded as that example, but they all held the energy of the underlying agreement and needed to be addressed. My connection to the cattle business was a sentimental attachment. I felt a huge obligation to my fathers to continue the legacy. My children had grown up loving life on the ranches. Being a cowman was a big part of my identity. That was where my personality and heart came together in my perception of myself. What I was faced with was separating sentimentality from the reality of the business. There was a lot of guilt around my behaviors the last few years of A.D.'s life. I wasted a lot of time I could have spent with him being hungover or burned out. I felt like I owed it to him to make the cattle company work, no matter what. But an attachment like that is a loaded gun. You carry it around with you, sometimes proud, sometimes ashamed, but always loaded. The crazy thing was that both men were dead. I would hope they were way beyond my letting them down.

Knowing what I knew and living what I knew were getting to be two different things. As I became more aware of the life I was creating for myself, I was put in the position of accepting total responsibility for my choices. If life was feeling great, it was my doing; the same was true if life felt tough. This awareness was still subject to all my judgments, the good-bad-right-wrong, going-to-punish-you-every-chance-I-get judge. I was beginning to question the judge's authority, but only beginning. I was grateful for how far my life had come in a couple of years.

✦ ✦ ✦

As time passed, I gave more and more of my time and energy to the Ranch. It looked like the Ranch Treatment Program would open in just a little over two years after I got out of treatment myself. That is unheard of in the recovery business. It seemed that the traditional recovery community believed that no recovering addict has anything to offer the world until he's been sober for at least two years. I was not interested in waiting two years, so I didn't. There were many unfavorable reactions to my being the owner of a treatment center. A huge value is placed on how many days you've been clean—*clean* being the number of days you've gone without a drink or a drug. The true quality of your life is secondary to the total score of clean days you've amassed.

Without the prerequisite number of clean days, I didn't qualify. That seemed insane to me. I was as humble as I could be, but I was still the guy with the go-to-hell attitude and more outspoken than smart. My introduction to being in the treatment business was by fire.

Evidently that's the only way I would have it because that's what I provoked. But I didn't get in the business for them.

I believed in a huge need for a broader-minded approach to recovery healing work. A lot of people were dying while trying to make the traditional recovery path work for them. That's all I needed to know.

I realized that the power in healing the wounds and beliefs that undermined our truth would allow each of us to live the "happy, joyous, and free" that life offers. Recovery is really about the power of personal responsibility and the grace of courage of compassion in action.

The Ranch existed because I was not alone in my commitment to creating a place of healing. My friends who led the equine workshops volunteered to serve on an advisory board, as did two of the professionals I'd met during treatment in Arizona. Through friends of friends, I was introduced to people who shared a passion for healing and recovery, and also had the clinical background and experience to serve the dream of the Ranch.

From the beginning I set the tone of diversity among the staff and contributors to the Ranch. I was not interested in everyone agreeing on how recovery should be defined or practiced. The Ranch was going to be a place where life was respected and supported in its transformation. The broader the perspectives of the staff, the more potential we had to connect with those searching for their truth.

As I experienced different healing processes, I introduced them to the clinical staff at the Ranch. They incorporated what they thought would make a contribution to our program. I had the best job of all. I got to be the guinea pig.

CHAPTER 12

Awakening, Initiation, and Gathering

My awakening began to snowball: The friends who had introduced me to *A Course in Miracles* also recommended the writings of the Zen Buddhist monk Thich Nhat Hanh, which I devoured. I began to read every thought-provoking, out-of-the-box book I could find—from Carlos Castaneda's Don Juan stories to Marianne Williamson, His Holiness the Dalai Lama, Thomas Mails' books on the Plains Indians, the Dead Sea Scrolls, the New Testament, and so on. I was hungry to see life as I hadn't yet experienced it, as if I had spent my whole life in a cage of limited perspectives and just realized that the door was unlocked.

My friends from Onsite Workshops (the company involved in the equine workshops) invited me to participate in several of their other amazing programs. My daughters and I attended their family program, which was a real miracle for us. It had been terrifying to face the truth of how my addictive behaviors had affected my children. In the workshops, they had the opportunity to talk to me face to face and tell me how they felt, including what they did and didn't like or trust about me. They had a voice and I got to listen. Around this time, I also met the coolest therapist, Lynde Stich, whose creative presence got me involved with a bimonthly group process that focused on finding answers from within.

✦ ✦ ✦

During one of the equine programs, I'd met a Diné man, Albert, a traditional Navajo healer. We connected immediately, and he invited me to a sweat lodge ceremony in Arizona. I took him up on the offer. This took no deliberation on my part, as I had learned by now that life was clever and spontaneous in its offering of opportunities to grow and heal, and I made a deal with myself that I would trust my feelings when a new opportunity came up and say yes if it felt right.

When I arrived at Albert's home for the ceremony, the sun was setting over the Tucson desert. To the north stood the Santa Catalina Mountains, the same mountains that had overlooked the treatment center and had shared many a dream with me. In the east, the moon was rising behind Mt. Lemmon. The sweat lodge stood—a dome of willows and string covered with blankets and tarps—in the chaparral behind Albert's home, with a fire burning in front of it. The door of the lodge faced east toward the rising moon and sun, a portal between the worlds. The door into the sweat lodge was thrown open and the shadows of the blazing fire danced across the front of the lodge.

By the time I arrived the fire had already been burning for a couple of hours. I could see, between the layers of wood and ash, the stones glowing with the heat and spirit of the fire. There was another native family there. They were Tohono O'odham, desert people: a father, mother, three young daughters, and the mother's sister. All were there to participate in this ceremony of prayer and cleansing.

I was excited, nervous, self-conscious, and willing. Somehow I was familiar with the space as if I'd been there before. I felt in tune with the frequency of the place; my spirit knew where we were. I had no idea what I was doing; I just knew in my heart that this opportunity was a gift. There was no special preparation other than not eating before and drinking lots of water. I had read about the lodge in *Black Elk Speaks,* but reading about it and being there were two different things.

Albert explained that we would do four "rounds." Each round— beginning in the east, moving to the south, then to the west, and finally the north—held a connection to the spirits and powers of the direction.

At the beginning of each round, the fire keeper brought in hot rocks from the fire pit outside into the shallow pit in the center of the lodge. Then, once the rocks had been placed and the door flap had been closed, Albert poured water over the hot rocks to create steam while we sang and prayed. While there was little concept of the passage of time, maybe twenty minutes to an hour had passed per round. I was literally shifting in and out of a greater dimension. Being in the presence of the Spirit and the elements in this way was all new to me. I felt so alive!

The power and presence of the ceremony was overwhelming. One second I'd feel so incredibly comfortable, and then the next I'd feel anxious. I saw and heard visions of jaguars and wolves in the soft glow of the stones; I could feel the air move like something was passing by my head in the darkness. In this place of total mystery, I was filled with love and gratitude. I experienced a depth of consciousness that was beyond my mind's understanding.

During the third round, a voice spoke to me, "Be in this place. Come here; you will find yourself here." I knew it. I believed it. It was the truth. The power of the heat and steam offered an awareness of surrender that moved through me. I could let go of everything in the lodge. I could let go of all that I believed about myself. I had discovered a doorway to freedom!

I would let go, over and over, through many lodges and in many places until all that would be left was the truth of my being.

After my first experience with the sweat lodge, I decided that this practice would become a regular part of my life as well as a part of the Ranch's offering to our clients. Bringing a sweat lodge into a treatment program was very controversial, but being me I really didn't care. This was about healing, not about the opinions of the professional treatment community. We built the lodge and the healing started immediately. We offered the lodges, and many of the Ranch clients had their deepest experiences in treatment in that sacred, hot, and sweaty place. Their experiences and why they had them in that setting is between them and God. It's nobody else's business. All I cared about was that it was helping people heal in a big way.

✦ ✦ ✦

Being an avid reader of all mind-opening books, I developed a love for bookstores. I liked to browse through the books and wait for something to catch my eye. On one of my bookstore journeys, *The Four Agreements* by don Miguel Ruiz jumped out at me. This book claimed to be based on the ancient teachings of the Toltec people. The Toltecs were the people of ancient Mexico known as "artists of the spirit." They had developed a way of looking at and being in life that bridged the physical and the spiritual. Carlos Castaneda's accounts of working with a Yaqui Indian Nagual, a sorcerer named Juan Matus, intrigued me. And because don Miguel Ruiz was a modern-day Nagual of Toltec lineage, I was equally intrigued.

As I read *The Four Agreements,* I was awed by its simple, yet pro-found approach to life and relationships. Something within the pages resonated deeply. What read as simple was, in actuality, very powerful. Four years of continuous reflection on myself, my life, my feeling of not fitting in, and wondering if I was on the right planet had given way to an understanding that reality is a matter of perception, and perception is subject to shifts in viewpoint.

We are conditioned to believe a certain way, and we become attached to it. We see the world through the eyes of opinion and judgment, believing that what we see is truth, all the while being completely asleep to the fact that what we see is our own beliefs, attitudes, opin-ions, and judgments reflected back at us. The practice of the Four Agreements gave me another grounding place, another way to live life aware of the nature and integrity of my choices, thoughts, and actions. Don Miguel's presentation of the knowledge of the Toltecs was so simple and clear, yet so deep and mind bending. From *Do Not Make Assumptions* and *Always Do Your Best* to *Be Impeccable with Your Word* and *Don't Take Anything Personally,* the Four Agreements gave me a very simple nonjudgmental guide to moment-to-moment living.

Not long after reading *The Four Agreements,* I received a newsletter from don Miguel's foundation. In the newsletter was a list of journeys to ancient sacred sites in Mexico and around the world. Mexico had always held a special allure, so I chose a trip to Teotihuacán (Teo). Teotihuacán translates as "the place where man awakens to God." It is home to the Pyramids of the Sun and Moon—the second largest pyramids on the planet.

The journey was being led by a couple who had years of experience working with don Miguel: Ted and Peggy Raess. I knew nothing of Teo. But intuition very gently and very deliberately pushed me to go. The intent of the trip was fascinating—five days of awakening and transcendence, a ceremony that had been practiced in Teo for thousands of years. I had no idea what would happen, but I was ready.

A couple of weeks before departure, Peggy called to connect and share with me that, by my intention to travel to Teotihuacán, I had set an energetic process in motion that I may not have been aware of. She suggested I take time to focus my awareness on what she called the dream of my life—all the relationships, attachments, obligations, agreements, and so on, basically everything in my life that I could reflect on.

The conversation seemed like it should have a little *woo-woo*—you know, *cosmic yah-yah*—but it didn't. There was a very sober awareness to it. In my conversation with Peggy, I was aware of a presence that was more than the two of us talking. I felt something that I couldn't explain. I told Peggy so, and she said, "That's it; that's perfect." She then said that, during the last week before the trip, I might want to say a silent good-bye to my life and the world as I've known it; nothing would be the same when I returned from Mexico.

All of this, just a couple of months before, would have been too much for the old surfing cowboy. There were voices in my head saying, "Bullshit! You gotta be kidding." I was going to Mexico anyway. My travel plan took me from Tennessee to Arizona, where I visited friends and connected with my Diné brother, Albert, for a purification sweat lodge ceremony. I wanted to be as clean and as grounded as possible. This journey was beginning to feel like I had opened a doorway to another dimension.

During the sweat lodge, I had a vision of two beady red eyes. Whether my eyes were opened or closed, those eyes were watching me. Inside the sweat lodge, it is pitch black, completely dark, except for the red-hot rocks. I was there in that timeless space, in the total darkness consumed by the intense heat and steam surrounded by the prayers and spirits of the lodge, having visions of a serpent watching me. I didn't recognize the serpent, but it seemed vaguely familiar, like pictures I had seen of ancient carvings in Central America.

During the third round of the lodge, Albert went outside and blew his eagle bone whistle. He was calling in the spirits of the four directions, praying for blessings on all in the lodge. As he blew the whistle outside, I felt the beating of wings and hot air pulsing as an invisible winged creature took flight. I closed my eyes to pray. I saw the head of the serpent transform into an eagle of pure light that rose from the stones in the center of the lodge and flew straight up into the darkness.

After the fourth and final round, I talked with Albert about my visions. I told him of the red eyes, the serpent, and how the serpent had become an eagle of light and had flown up and out of the lodge.

Albert smiled at me. "I know," he said. "They will be waiting for you in Mexico."

CHAPTER 13

The Pilgrimage

The view of Mexico from the plane's window filled me with awe. I looked down on another world and wondered about the lives below. I'd always felt an attraction to Mexico, and I silently mused that maybe this journey would be the fulfillment of some past-life experience or obligation.

When I passed through customs into the main airport, I was suddenly struck by an otherworldly feeling. As I blended into the flow of people moving down the halls, I felt alive and grateful to be there. I was in a different land, but, at the same time, I felt like I was home and exactly where I was supposed to be.

I had been told to meet with the group at a small cantina in the airport just outside the customs area, the Freedom Café. Here I would be introduced to the leaders of this adventure. I'd never traveled so far to connect with people I didn't know, but then I wasn't really there to meet them; I was in this place looking for me.

It was no coincidence that we were meeting at a joint called the Freedom Café to begin this journey. Freedom had become my mission in life. I had found the grace and support of the recovery world, but I was not interested in taking permanent refuge there. As the tapestry of my life unraveled, I'd realized that the world I had been taught to believe in was not real for me either. My idea of freedom was growing just a touch faster than whatever my present state of mind was. Freedom was always just beyond my ability to define it, and I was tired of definitions.

As I stood in the hallway of the Mexico City Airport, I realized that there wasn't a single person in the 26 million people in Mexico City who knew me from the man in the moon. I was just me. *This* was freedom. I had done it. I had stepped out of tired, dull, self-indulgent old me into the space of something else. God, I felt alive. The hallway outside customs was a steady flow of humanity—business suits, tourists, Indian peoples in native dress, gringos, *federales*; this was showtime.

To my right, I saw the sign for the Freedom Café. Ted and Peggy stood just outside the door to the café. Ted was a big guy, six-foot-two, 220 pounds; he wore a felt fedora and a welcome-home grin. With red hair and blue eyes, Peggy literally beamed with warmth. I liked them at first sight, and we exchanged hugs and made our introductions. Next, they introduced me to the group of more than a dozen.

While we waited for one more member of our group to arrive, I bought a Cuban cigar and stepped outside. As the rich smoke curled around my head, I thought about all I had seen and done over the last few years. I had no regrets, no doubts. It had taken all of that to be the guy standing there on that curb smoking that cigar. I realized I was comfortable being me, and I knew what a gift that realization was. Most of all, I was aware that I was only beginning to get to know myself.

Halfway through my cigar, it was time to leave for Teo. There were sixteen people in our group—ten women and six men—all intent on this journey into the heart of antiquity. Scanning the faces of my companions, I noticed several attractive ladies. I smiled inwardly; some things never change. Sure, my attention was on the magic of the journey, but I was still a single male on tour.

We gathered our bags and headed down the hall behind Frederico, the transportation maestro from our hotel. He looked like he could have been the brother of the Mexican Revolutionary general Pancho Villa. When he first approached, I caught him eyeing the ladies, too. We gave each other a knowing nod, and he whispered, "Hola, coyote. Que tal?" I didn't need to know the exact translation to understand the message from one coyote to another.

Our group climbed onto the small bus that would take us to Teo, which was about an hour away. I felt in my gut that I was truly moving toward my destiny. The ride through Mexico City uncovered a colorful tapestry of humanity constantly being woven and unwoven by a whirlwind of activity. I loved it. Once we passed the city limits, sights that were familiar to me became more common: alfalfa fields, livestock trucks, and small plots of land being farmed by hand. We passed a school for charros, the amazing horsemen and ropers of Mexico. As we moved farther from town, the countryside became a patchwork of fields and villages. The sky was a beautiful blue with clouds hanging over the mountains surrounding the valley of Mexico. In the distance, I saw and smelled a rain shower moving slowly across the valley.

I felt the land. I felt the struggle of life there. I saw it in the faces of the people. I saw hardship in their eyes along with a determination to survive. I saw faith and the power of life. These people looked alive to me in a way that most Americans don't. Our standard of living has come at a high price; we've given up our relationship with our souls for the sake of *more*.

As we drove, I kept looking beyond the fields for a glimpse of the pyramids. When the driver took the exit to the "Pyramides Teotihuacán," my heart jumped, and my whole being pulsed with electricity.

✦ ✦ ✦

The Pyramid of the Moon rose in the distance. We took another turn, and I saw the Pyramid of the Sun, the temple to the Creator through which all life passes to earth. Everything became still. I knew this place.

After pulling into the parking lot of our little hotel, I climbed out of the bus and turned to look back. I stared down the Avenue of the Dead. Before me were the Pyramids of the Sun and Moon, and the Temple of Quetzalcoatl, the plumed serpent who transcended earth to fly as an eagle. I flashed back to the vision from the sweat lodge and time stopped. This dream encompassed the past, present, and future.

As I looked down the avenue at the pyramids, tears began to flow. This made no sense to me. Why was I so overwhelmed? How did I know this place?

Ted walked up behind me and asked if I was all right. I tried to speak, but couldn't. He smiled, patted me on the back, and said, "Welcome home, brother. It's been a long time."

CHAPTER 14

Dreamtime

My arrival in Teo was the most powerful feeling of familiarity and connection I'd ever felt. This was no ordinary déjà vu experience, where I'd felt some connection to land or water. Here, I felt as if I were two people who were separated by a millennium, both seeing through my eyes in the same moment. To have the feelings of this lifetime were plenty. To experience feelings I had no conscious relationship to both scared and excited me. My body felt like a supercomputer, processing more information than ever before. I felt an incredible expansion of awareness. But, surprisingly, I was comfortable with it.

I heard Peggy call me. Her voice brought me back into the present. Looking around, I was impressed with the beauty of our little hotel, the Villa Archeologica. Giant yuccas and bird-of-paradise plants stood proudly among the magueys and cactus. The buildings were alive with color—blue and red and lavender and orange. In the courtyard, an open-air pool surrounded by palms and flowering bougainvillea lay in wait.

The staff set up a welcome reception for us. Margaritas and fruit punch, guacamole and fresh tortilla chips, and hugs and smiles for everybody. It literally felt like a welcome-home gathering. Once we were settled, we had a meeting with Ted and Peggy. I felt so at ease with them, but I was not ready to talk about my connection to this place. What felt comfortable in my body sounded crazy in my head, which was a complete flip from all the years of living what was okay in my head but not okay in my body.

My first night was a dream fest; it reminded me of treatment. I was in the right place, but I was not sure who I was anymore. I had to focus on my identity to feel comfortable in my skin. That first morning as I ordered *desayuno* (breakfast), Peggy asked how I slept.

"Pretty crazy," I replied.

"Did you dream?" she asked.

I looked up at her through a fog. "Oh yeah, I spent the night with one of those statues. I think they're called *chacmools*? I can't really tell you what went on that would actually make sense now, but I have a connection to this world of pyramids and magic; it is definitely working me."

I wanted Peggy to explain what I was experiencing or help me interpret it, but all I could get out of her was, "That's perfect," and, "Yes, you are connected to this place."

Looking back, I now know that I had been introduced to the layers of time and space—the dreams of all humanity, which were at one time what we call reality. Although they no longer exist in the same form today, they remain.

✦ ✦ ✦

Being in Teotihuacán was my invitation to wake up to the realms beyond what I had been taught to believe in. My identity was based

on all the agreements I had made in life, which don Miguel Ruiz
calls domestication. I was beginning to remember that I was the life
force that flowed through my body, not the identity that labeled me.
My mind was not comfortable with this multiple-reality thing, so I
was hit with a mild state of confusion. The difference between my
confusion at that moment and my past feelings of confusion was the
sense of peace that felt so close. Peace and confusion had never come
together before, and yet here they were.

I understood that confusion. This experience reminded me of
treatment with a dose of magic thrown in. I was digging this. After
my experience of having been labeled, diagnosed, assessed, and cat-
egorized, Teotihuacán felt like a midnight reprieve from the governor.
I had had my share of suffering by definition. If cracking reality was
going to help me undo my life of fear and judgment, then bring it on.

✦   ✦   ✦

After breakfast we gathered in front of our hotel. We received an
outline of the day's events. To begin, we would walk the mile or so to
the front gates leading into the grounds of Teo. A blue sky and the clear
crisp air of the high desert made a walk sound great. Then, we were asked
to choose a partner for the walk. As Ted explained, we'd be walking in
pairs, and one of us would be blindfolded, while the other would watch
out for our safety. The point was to feel our bodies, trust, and allow our
awareness to expand. Teo had been created to broaden awareness—to
be the place where humans awaken to our divinity. In Teotihuacán,
awareness is the key to enlightenment. I had never seen the power of
awareness from such a clear perspective. Judgment did not apply.

All my years of insanity—the drinking, the drugging, the lady-
loving—had always been about shifting my awareness away from
myself and onto some altered state or other person. I dedicated myself
to what I had been taught, but that type of fulfillment comes from

what we do or accomplish, not from what we are. In my old view of awareness, there had been an underlying fear of the truth. I was now being offered awareness as the key to reclaiming my power of choice. The life I had lived had been the result of my choosing, but now I was being offered the opportunity to see how I could use the power of choice to redefine my destiny.

Once we passed through the gates, we were eye to eye with the Temple of Quetzalcoatl. Straight ahead was the Avenue of the Dead. The Pyramid of the Sun stood to my left, and off in the distance, at the far end of the Avenue of the Dead, resided the Pyramid of the Moon.

I'd felt very centered on the walk over. Walking without sight had shifted my awareness from the chatter in my head to a place of pure feeling. As I looked across the way at the Temple of Quetzalcoatl, my perception shifted to a dreamlike state. Each step upward toward the Temple of Quetzalcoatl reminded me of my intention for being there. No longer on a simple adventure, I absolutely knew this place, and this place knew me. I had returned to remember.

At the top of the steps we looked out across a large plaza. A raised platform built of stone and dirt stood in the center. Suddenly, I had a vision of a group of priests addressing a crowd from the platform. They wore bright ceremonial garments adorned with plumes and feathers that caught the light and danced in the breeze. I was among them. I was one of them. My entire being was a state of pure unconditional love. I was home. In that flash I understood the feeling I had been missing and longing for. A part of me had remembered that feeling— a memory of connection I felt in my body; it was one of being the brightest, warmest light imaginable. The flash lasted only a moment, yet it gave me an awareness that challenged my concept of life and consciousness. Not remembering the source of that light and love resulted in anxiety; my mind wanted an address.

Once more, I found myself awake in the dream. As otherworldly as this experience seemed to be, it felt natural. I had no need to react. Deep inside I knew that I had just reconnected with myself through a bridge that spanned time.

✦ ✦ ✦

This first plaza in our process was known as the Plaza of Hell—the beginning point on our journey to reclaim awareness and integrity. To change where I was, I first needed to *know* where I was—to see and feel and accept it.

We spent the morning recapitulating our lives, identifying our beliefs and perceptions. I had done a lot of recapitulation on my behaviors, but I had never considered that my entire belief system might be in need of a thorough examination. The voices in my head picked up on the conversation of my definition of me as a recovering person. "My name's Lee and I'm an addict." That was an absolute in the recovery world's price of admission.

I had not believed that shallow definition, but my disbelief had been set in fear. The fear was a reflection of my lack of faith in myself. I didn't like me, so how could I believe in me? At the same time, I was not willing to go along with what was demanded of me just to fit in. This Plaza of Hell was filled with all those voices and fears, with all the shame and guilt of my past and all the prayers and hope that I would find a way out.

As I followed Peggy and Ted's direction to pick up rocks that would represent what I would let go of in my life, I stopped and looked around at the beauty that surrounded me. How could I feel so dark and challenged and be surrounded by such beauty? I lived in a production of contradictions, and I was the main character.

✦ ✦ ✦

From the Plaza of Hell, we moved on to the Temple of Quetzalcoatl. It was bone dry, but, in my mind, water filled the place. As we entered the temple, I could feel its presence. Entering the mouth of the temple was a metaphor for entering the mouth of the avatar Quetzalquatal, the two-headed serpent, the body of Teotihuacán.

Our group sat on steps that ran up the west side of the temple, and we faced an array of stone carvings of Quetzalquatal and his co-creating God Tlaloc, which were mounted on the east wall. Those stone carvings had stood vigil there for more than a thousand years. I wondered what they had witnessed in their time. I thought about all the people who had come for all their many reasons to gaze into the eyes of Life.

I knew then that I had come to let go. Whatever that meant, I would do that, having no idea of what letting go would look like. Peggy asked us to gaze into the mouths of the stone carvings and feel the stones and walls surrounding us as they breathed in and out with us—one body, one breath, one life.

Ted then told us the story of the ancient masters who would bring their apprentices to this place in the ceremony of commitment that would allow the apprentices to move into the deepest level of teachings that the Toltec mystery school held.

He said, "To move beyond this place you have to be willing to let go of all you have come to believe you are. You have to have absolute faith in life, in the one that created you, that you will be led back to the truth of your divinity. It is you that denies yourself freedom, the freedom that life offers without conditions, the freedom of unconditional love. Are you willing to make that commitment to yourself? Are you willing to let go, to see the truth with no expectations? Are you willing to die to the life that you have known, so that you might really live?"

I was, and, without knowing what I was really asking for, I did.

CHAPTER 15

From Survival to Expansion

In this ancient place, my path to recovery shifted from survival to expansion. I was becoming conscious of my awareness and saw that my perception was being projected onto the world, rather than the reverse.

Perception is experienced as it occurs in the moment. The reaction to that perception can go on for seconds, moments, or years, possibly for generations. Realizing that I was waking up to the way humanity projected its dream, our dream, I felt responsible for this awareness. For all my craziness, for the years of living like a madman, somehow I had put myself where I could feel the truth.

Life is amazing! How could all that belief in judgment, of hell and damnation, be for real, when a nut like me gets so many chances? In the Temple of Quetzalcoatl, we faced the reality of commitment to ourselves.

We were told the story of how the apprentices of ancient Teotihuacán were given the choice to trust their teachers and take the ultimate leap of faith or not. There was no shame or judgment—just the choice.

That is life, isn't it? To either choose from the heart what we aspire to or settle for the world's version of what we would be if we are willing to believe that something outside of ourselves would know better than we do. After having believed that life was a great maze, I now found myself in more of a labyrinth. A labyrinth leads back to the center rather than to the outside, as a maze does. It was my center that I had been missing.

From the Temple of Quetzalcoatl, we moved onto the Avenue of the Dead. Off in the distance, the Pyramid of the Moon stood awaiting our arrival. We had entered a space of timelessness. The journey of Teotihuacán is a journey of unraveling—of our pasts, our beliefs, our behaviors, of all that would serve to bind us to what we knew before to what we believed was reality—the reality that fed our suffering.

We crossed the River San Juan, a muddy stream. The river flows east to west across the Avenue of the Dead. Crossing a river is a metaphor in many different mythologies; the Styx, the Ganges, the Nile, the Jordan, and, of course, the mighty Mississippi, separating the known territory of the east from the wilderness of the west.

This was still the first day in Teo, and I was realizing that, in the many metaphors Ted and Peggy were using in their teachings, I was allowed to see how awareness as well as knowledge could be communicated through metaphor. The beauty of this filled me up.

Most of my life I had heard metaphors taken literally with no room or tolerance for personal interpretation. This was just the opposite. Because we would be the ones learning through metaphors, we were challenged to listen to ourselves for the deeper meanings that would be revealed from within. The teachers were teaching from a place of respect for us as students and as people. I was not being told; rather, I was being guided to see for myself.

Their style of teaching was a practice in taking responsibility for the results of my choosing, while at the same time seeing how I automatically judged myself for those choices. This truly was a fertile ground for the evolution of awareness. To cross the river meant you were willing to break from the known and walk with faith into a new life. It takes courage to make that break. It takes all of those things that people in recovery hear about, and it takes trusting life and yourself.

At the Rio San Juan, I turned to look back at my past. What has been has been, and that's that. I said to all that lay behind me that I was grateful. I looked down into the river, asking the water for the resilience to go on. Newly emerged butterflies flew up all around the bridge we stood on. Sometimes there is no room for doubt. I found faith, hope, and joy in the first flights of the butterflies—happy, joyous, and free.

Overhead, the sky shone the beautiful blue I'd seen reflected in my little girls' eyes. It was "the Day of the Lord, when the divinity returns to us." We were living what Teotihuacán had been created for.

✦ ✦ ✦

Beyond the river is a series of plazas, each dedicated to a particular element and aspect of our experience. I had always wanted to be a big boss, and I was beginning to realize that I could be a much bigger boss than I had ever imagined. I could be the boss of my own experience in life.

My life was my creation. Whatever that experience was, I was responsible for that production. I couldn't control all events, but I was absolutely responsible for my reaction to them. I began to understand that reactions to life were a choice, not a law. Just as I had learned how to behave from my parents and the world around me, I could unlearn those behaviors that no longer served me.

Over the next two days we moved through those plazas along the Avenue of the Dead to the altar in front of the Pyramid of the Moon.

Plaza of Earth

The first plaza we entered was earth, the realm of the physical body, the manifestation of this lifetime. To move on in life, I had to first be willing to bury all the structure that I had come to define myself by. Earth is where I created my structure, so earth is where I would let it go. Ted and Peggy told us to preside over our own funerals. The directions were simple. First of all, I'd invite everyone I wanted to attend.

With my eyes closed I saw the faces of all the people in my life that I would want to celebrate my burial. There were friends and family, some family still alive and some who were on the other side waiting for me. Then I selected the music and food to be served at my death ceremony. I could hear David Crosby singing, "Almost cut my hair." The soundtrack of my life was rocking the clouds overhead. The food was fried venison and grits, the stuff I had grown up with. As my imagined gathering came together with all my gratitude, I buried the oyster shell that had appeared on the grounds to serve as my body. How an oyster shell got to the Plaza of Earth in the middle of central Mexico was beyond me, and it was also perfect. I had grown up on oysters and beer and had cut tires and feet on the oyster shell roads around the beach towns of north Florida.

The burial ceremony was a powerful process that cannot be conveyed in words. It is one to be experienced. Through this experience, you, too, can find what you are looking for.

Plaza of Water

Next we went to the Plaza of Water. We are born into this world through water. The embryo grows and develops in the watery world of the womb. The Plaza of Water was our place of cleansing and releasing all that goes against our free relationship with life. All my life, water had been my place of nurturing. From surfing and scuba diving in the oceans, to walking and fishing in the creeks and rivers of the mountains and valleys, I always felt closer to home by the water. Water is the element of emotion. Our bodies are 97 percent water.

Sitting on the steps looking across the Plaza of Water, I listened to Peggy speak of the relationship to our emotional body. What I was hearing reflected the interaction between my emotions and my reactions. I had always accepted my emotional reactions as justified. Anger, fear, sadness, joy—I had never considered that I might be more responsible for how I react to my emotions. If I was really going to call myself an adult, I was going to have to be an adult in my relationship with my emotions. My awareness expanded again, and, rather than judge myself over the past, I felt excited about how I could change my life by being responsible for my emotional reactions.

At the close of her teaching, Peggy led us down the steps and into the energy of our imagined water-filled plaza. I was dreaming water with my eyes open—feeling it, loving it, allowing the water to flow through me, and giving all my gratitude to the oceans and rivers that had been my places of comfort and solitude throughout my life. I was a walking prayer of gratitude and excitement for what might lie ahead.

Plaza of Air

Beyond water is the Plaza of Air. Air is the element of mind. The light of creation passes from the sun through air into water to be manifest as the body and blood of humanity—of life on Earth. In the Plaza of Air, we expose the deepest wounds of our being.

As we shared our stories, Ted and Peggy reflected for us how invested we were in our stories being the truth. They asked us to consider questioning the validity of our stories. Were they really the truth or possibly just what we had created from the original experience and called the truth?

This plaza was also the realm over which the mind presided. Not the brain, the mind, with all its knowledge and power of reason. It is the mind that is the story creator and the aspect of our being that will decide for us what the truth is if left unchallenged. The problem with that setup is that what the mind knows is its interpretation of our experiences, and those interpretations are subject to our judgments, opinions, and old agreements about what we believe to be the truth. The result is that these stories are not being projected onto a "clean screen." Our stories are distorted by our investment in the past, in being right or wrong, and in the filters that arise from our belief in opinions and judgments.

The point of view shared by our guides was an introduction to the Toltec mystery school in action. The perception felt true, but I couldn't just accept it. That would have been too simple. My reaction to the teaching—to what the Toltecs called silent knowledge—sent tremors through my understanding of how I thought I worked as a person. I say "thought I worked" because at the same time I knew I didn't have a clue how I worked. Still, I was resistant to this new point of view.

The difference between processing emotions in Teotihuacán and processing them in similar group experiences was that here we had our teachers' awareness and their ability to awaken that within each one of us as well. To process the emotions connected to our wounds without knowing that we possess the ability to completely release the energy of those emotions back into the light of creation blocks our ability to free ourselves from our own self-perpetuated hell. We even have a term for it: *baggage* or *shadow side*. The ironic thing is that we do it to ourselves, and then project the blame or our excuses onto everything around us. It is our own beliefs that bind us to our suffering. We created that belief system; we can re-create it.

As my awareness expanded, my justifications for accepting that I was less than I could be began to disintegrate. I was faced with the choice of pity or power. So tired of my old broken-down tape of whining lies, I made the commitment to take responsibility for everything in my life.

An island of stone sits in the center of the Plaza of Air. As I sat praying, opening my heart to the Creator, I realized that the stones around me were breathing. Deep within that structure of rock, I felt a heartbeat. I was waking up.

Plaza of Fire

The next plaza was fire, life force, and Spirit. We had made a progression from the denseness of earth, through water, to air, and now Spirit in fire; our path of unraveling had led us to the source of our being. It is Spirit that animates these bodies. It is Spirit that perceives through the distortions of our belief systems. In Spirit, we come and go in this world. The Plaza of Fire was the place of the final cleansing.

In the truth, there is a calm, peaceful presence within each of us. Regardless of what is going on around us, when we are one with ourselves, we are still inside. In the Plaza of Fire, I felt the shadows of all that I still clung to. My lack of true faith claimed to offer a better deal than the truth. But this was not Judgment Day. As I examined myself, I felt self-compassion, knowing I was doing my best.

Fire consumes; it converts energy from one form to another. In the sweat lodge, fire feeds on the energy of the wood heating the stones. The wood is transformed into heat, light, and ash. The stones are then carried into the lodge where the energy of the fire heats the air and transforms the water that is poured on the rocks into the cleansing steam that bathes our bodies.

During my life I had woven an amazing safety net that, in truth, was a net of fears. It was time for me to give my safety net to the fire. My freedom lay in learning the lessons of faith. Walking toward the steps leading out of the Plaza of Fire, I felt so completely present in my body and so free from the confusion of my mind that time, once again, stood still. I was alive, walking a path that had held the intent of transformation for two thousand years.

For all my questions and doubts, I moved forward. Through my own intent, I was giving back to life what had always belonged to life, *me*, and I was seeing how I had held myself apart from life and freedom out of believing what the world demands from us, that we fear anything beyond what we are taught is right and real. To fear a God of unconditional love is ridiculous, and I was realizing that I had never feared God. What I had feared was the world of men.

That is the fear that I would leave for the fire. It would take many times of leaving this fear behind, and, on each of those offerings, I would reclaim another piece of my faith in myself and my Creator. This plaza in Teotihuacán held the fire of redemption, the fire of Moses and the burning bush, the fire of truth that doesn't require our believing in it for it to continue burning, awaiting our return to ourselves.

The Plaza of Recollection

Stepping up and out of the Plaza of Fire, I looked across to the one final plaza that lay between me and the avenue that led to the Pyramids of the Moon and Sun. This was the Plaza of Recollection, the place of recalling, of recapitulating my journey through life. The last few days felt like a lifetime. Recollection is for the owning of all of this lifetime. Not clinging to the experiences, simply seeing, feeling, witnessing, and saying thank you for all of it. To let go of living in judgment, it is necessary to stop judging.

Our group gathered on the steps at the south end of the plaza. Ted and Peggy asked us to close our eyes and see ourselves as we had arrived in Mexico City. Peggy said, "Remember the excitement and anxiety of arriving at the airport, wondering what might lie ahead. See yourself getting on the van headed here to Teo. Retrace your steps to this point, to this moment, embrace who you are now, with all the awareness that has awakened within you. See yourself in the light of your truth today."

As I followed their guidance, I was overwhelmed with gratitude. I was not the same person who got on the plane to Mexico City. What I knew to be different did not need to be explained or justified. What I knew to be different was my truth—and that was between life itself and me. There was no need for agreement or validation from anyone else.

Ted then asked us to see ourselves walking beside our energetic doubles. This double was pure unmanifest energy. We were to fill the double with all the memories, beliefs, feelings, judgments, fears—all that we could identify as a part of ourselves. We were going to walk from our starting point at the north end of the Plaza of Recollection to the altar at the Pyramid of the Moon. As we walked, this double would grow, until it was as huge as the universe. Then, at the altar of the moon, the double would shrink down to an egg of pure energy, the same size as our physical bodies.

My mind immediately started chattering about how silly all of this sounded. I walked anyway. I did my best to fill my double with all that made Lee Lee. Standing on our right, to the east side of the Avenue of the Dead, the Pyramid of the Sun rose up, as if it were a great generator of energy. As I passed in front of the Pyramid of the Sun, my attention was pulled up onto the face of this incredible temple to life. For a moment I became distracted and laughed at my flimsy control over my attention. I stopped, closed my eyes, and redirected my awareness back to feeding my double.

CHAPTER 16

Resonating with My Heart

B y the time I reached the altar in front of the Pyramid of the Moon, my entire being vibrated from the energy of my huge double. Peggy led us to the center of the raised platform that was the altar to the moon. Two men and two women were placed in the center, sitting back to back, facing in the four directions. I was told to sit in front of a beautiful woman named Dana. We had become true friends during this time together. Looking in her eyes was like looking into the heart of all I might dream of in a lover and a friend.

As the rest of our group was positioned, we were instructed to open our hearts as wide as we could and then a little more. We were directed to close our eyes, focusing on a channel of energy that would flow from our hearts to the hearts of those in the center. The four sitting in the center were told to open their hearts to receive and, at the same time, to open a channel at the crown of their heads that would allow all the energy fed into them to flow back to the sun.

We were going to offer up all that we had fed into the doubles, giving back to God what was God's. To let go of all that we have come to believe we are is to accept the Creator's intent for us. No fear, no doubt. All it takes is faith. As the channels opened and the connections were made, my awareness expanded like a light through the shadows. I was feeling Dana as though we were one being. As our energy bodies came together, I felt as though I was merging with all of creation. I was aware of my physical body sitting on the altar in front of the Pyramid of the Moon, and I could feel the power of my being flowing through Dana.

In that moment, I experienced the most incredible peace and joy. Every cell in my body was resonating with the energy of my heart and the light of the sun. I was in love with the universe. The further I went into the expansion, the faster the transitions came. I began to see colors, a soft blue, then green, violet, pink, and finally the softest brightest white light imaginable. I heard someone nearby speaking, but I had no interest in voices, or what they were saying. I was truly in two places at once.

My physical body had not moved from the spot where I first sat down, but at the same time my awareness was streaming through realms of creation that I never knew existed. The experience lasted maybe twenty minutes, and, at the same time, it seemed like it went on forever. In those moments on the Altar of the Moon, I consciously touched the Infinite.

As my awareness shifted back to my physical body, I lay on the ground, looking up at the sky. My mind was completely still. In that moment I knew that life was eternal. I knew that I was okay. What I had just experienced was who I really am. There was no story; no need to know that would interfere with what had passed through me. I had just experienced home, where we come from; all the king's horses and all the king's men could not take that away from me again.

My perception was no longer trapped within my physical senses or in my mind. When I sat up and looked around, I was overwhelmed with love for life. The beauty of the light fed me like sleep feeds the dreamer. I had just connected the bridge between heaven and earth. The serpent had flown like the eagle.

I watched as Peggy helped Dana get grounded into her body. Dana was glowing with the white light of my vision. As I reached out and took her hand, I suddenly was there again, in the light, filled with an unconditional love beyond words. We hugged, not needing to say anything, sharing all that we were.

Day three of this journey to heaven on earth slowly shifted back to the world of the physical. We gathered our things and walked down the steps from the altar to the realm of humanity, the dream of the planet.

Ted came up behind Dana and said, "Let's get some ice cream."

Off we went to the world of vendors and souvenirs. The beauty and joy of life was all around us. I guess it had always been there. I had just forgotten how to see it. Absolute freedom came from having my awareness shifted beyond my mind's control. Realizing that I had always held the key to my own personal freedom, with no awareness of it, was suddenly very funny. All those years of frustration, fear, and hesitation had been my graduate work in illusion. I felt no regret, only gratitude.

The greatest gift was accepting that my willingness to not settle for someone else's version of good enough and to keep searching beyond all judgments had brought me to my authenticity. What I had craved through all the searching was the real me.

After our ice cream break, we climbed the Pyramid of the Moon. I looked out across the valley of Teotihuacán, down the Avenue of the Dead to the Pyramid of the Sun and the Temple of Quetzalcoatl.

Everything I saw was a reflection of life and creation. This journey of only a few days had become my experience of transformation. What I saw looking out from the Pyramid of the Moon was not the same as what I had seen the day we arrived.

I felt my surroundings moving, flowing, and breathing with the heartbeat of the earth. There were no thoughts. My third day in Mexico had become my day of resurrection. Reality had found its way through to me. It was much more than I could have ever believed. Somewhere off in the distance I saw myself as a thirteen-year-old kid listening to the Woodstock soundtrack and Richie Havens wailing, "Freedom, freedom, freeeedommmmm."

That afternoon I went back to the hotel for a swim. I sat on the bottom for as long as I could. There is a Lakota Sioux prayer we use in the sweat lodge, *Mitakuye Oyasin* (which translates as "all my relations"—meaning that all of creation is related through the Creator of all things). We are all of one source. Sitting on the bottom of the pool, I was all my relations.

That night we gathered to share our experiences of the day. Every time I looked at Dana I was in LOVE—not the love of "I need you, baby." This was the love that is more than words or touch. I was in love with everything around me, including me. Because Dana had been the first person I'd put my attention on during our experience on the Altar of the Moon, I guess my mind decided the experience was because of her. Of course I knew it was much greater than that, but she was so beautiful that letting it be about her was easy. However, there was a great awareness in my reaction. All of my life I had given the power of feeling love away to someone or something outside me. I saw this now.

What I was feeling this time was that the feelings were coming from within me, for me. This was a whole new expression of love in my life. In fact, this was the beginning of the realization that life *was* love's presence. The two concepts had been separated by definition and teaching; that point of view was the way humanity had decided to see love and life and was not the truth of either.

Palace of the Butterflies

The next morning I awoke at 4:00 AM. Between the energy of the physical process and the mind's reactions to expansion of consciousness, my body had only catnapped through the night. Early morning in Teo is beautiful. Hundreds of finches live in the giant agaves in front of the hotel. At sunrise they all come to life, singing and chasing their breakfast through the morning light.

This was our last day, the day we would climb the Pyramid of the Sun. Sitting in front of the hotel, watching the birds, I felt torn between two worlds. One was the world I had come from, my own personal history; the other was the world I perceived in that moment. My awareness was so alive and open to the life around me, I felt more awake than I could ever remember. I felt sadness for all that had been and huge excitement for what could be. I didn't want to leave Teo. But the gift of Teo is to return to my world with this spark of awareness. I began to understand what Ted and Peggy meant when they said we were all messengers of light. We are Light, the Light of the World. Through the Light, information is conveyed; through the light, our DNA is transferred into this world. Quantum physics now realizes that all creation is a manifestation of varying densities and frequencies of Light. When we move back into our center as beings, as humans, we once again have a conscious awareness of the Light and wisdom of our Spirit.

After breakfast we gathered, as we did every day, in front of the hotel. We were told that we would walk to the farthest gate, the one near the Pyramid of the Moon, and that we would walk in silence. On each successive day, we had walked away from the familiar world into a world of reflection and awareness. Through ceremony and intent, we had peeled layer after layer of belief and experience, gaining as much clarity and freedom as we could accept. Intensity had built to a point of release.

I had the eerie feeling that today held something special, and so I walked in silence. When we reached the entrance to the grounds, Ted reminded us to stay silent. He said that we were going into a place known as the Palace of the Butterflies, Quetzalpapalotl. If the energy of love can be manifest in a physical location, it has been in the Palace of the Butterflies.

Palace of Quetzalpapalotl

In the Palace of Quetzalpapalotl, grace has made a home for us. I sat on a step that led into the small courtyard of the palace. As I watched, Peggy worked with different people. Sitting there, I gently slipped into a waking dream. I was in another time sitting in this same spot, but this time it was night, and the courtyard of the plaza was filled with water. Overhead was a sky full of stars, all reflecting in the water. As I looked at my hands, I realized they were the hands of a much older man. I wasn't startled, just interested. I was absolutely at peace and more intrigued by the light on the water than by this overlap in time.

The night felt cool and completely still. I realized that I could see the light beams of the moon penetrating through the air. As I focused on the moonlight, my physical body began to disintegrate. I became particles of light merging with the rays of moonlight.

I was pulled back into present time by Dana's hand on my shoulder. She looked into my eyes, smiling.

I said, "God, I love you, girl."

The words were spoken without thought or need. She led me into the center of the courtyard, where Peggy asked me to stand over a small hole that was the axis of the courtyard. Dana stood in front of me. Eye to eye, we gazed into the depths of our being. I felt the same sensation as my dream of merging with the moonlight.

Peggy's voice said, "All you're feeling is you. This is who you really are, and this is what you are here to share through this life. You are love, you are light."

Then I was gone again, merging with all the love that filled this Palace of Quetzalpapalotl. As I lay on the ground, feeling the sun on my face, I opened my eyes to the blue of heaven's sky. I was no longer sure who I was and did not really care. I knew what I had never truly believed before: I was okay.

Palace of the Jaguars

Leaving the palace, we walked down stone steps leading to a series of rooms beneath the Palace of the Butterflies. My time and space paradigm was whacked. One moment I was Lee, the next I was an old native man of antiquity, living in this place called the Palace of the Jaguars. My entire physical form changed. The way I walked, the way I responded to feelings or people, came from two different perspectives. My mind wanted to freak out, but I was too comfortable in my body for that to happen. The time I spent in the Palace of the Jaguars was as comfortable as my dad's kitchen used to be. It felt like home.

We were told how the old priests of ancient Teotihuacán lived here until it was time for them to leave their physical bodies. In the world of the ancient Toltecs, students of life worked to become masters of personal experience. Once the masters merged with the unmanifest in Spirit, they are able to leave their body at will. Deep within the rooms of the palace complex were portals, doorways that these ancient masters could pass through. They could literally travel, fully conscious, from place to place through these energetic doorways, sort of like using a sci-fi transporter. But these masters didn't need a machine to transit. At the end of their time in the physical world, the old ones simply stood, facing the portal, and jumped out of their body, merging with the pure light of creation.

We each took our turn facing the portal. It is said the energy of the portal is the energy of the Christ, the energy of the Enlightened Ones. What I felt in that place was the presence of pure love. I cannot explain my concept of God any better than that. How do you attach an identity to the infinite?

I did not leave the Palace of the Jaguars alone. I was still Lee, the guy who had booked the trip, but I was joined by the spirit of the one I was with in the courtyard of the butterflies.

This was the final leg of our journey. We were going to the top of the Pyramid of the Sun. As I looked out at the world around me, I became aware of dual perceptions. Two personalities looked through my eyes. I walked differently. My legs bowed like an old cowboy's. Everything I saw, felt, or thought passed through the consciousness of two personalities. Looking at the people walking the avenue, my awareness was much broader than Lee's.

Pyramid of the Sun

When we reached the Pyramid of the Sun, I stopped to look up. I quietly told myself that, if the spirit of the old one would guide me, I would do the work. I offered up my heart, my mind, my body, and my spirit to the will of the Creator.

We gathered at the altar in front of the Pyramid of the Sun. We were given directions for our walk up to the top. Our group was split into male and female. We formed lines that climbed to each level

together, then separated, the men going left, the women right. We
came back together to climb to the next level, repeating the pattern
until we reached the top. We crisscrossed in the pattern of DNA.

At each corner of the pyramid I stopped to honor the four directions, offering all of me back to the Creator. Walking the levels is an
incredible experience. It's not like a sidewalk. The rough stones have
been bound together to make the pyramid, and good hiking boots are
useful here. But the views at the corners of the pyramid are amazing.
The builders of the Pyramid of the Sun thought they had built the
largest building in the world. Except for the Great Pyramid at Giza,
they were right, but that one is not built to climb on the outside.
Twenty-five hundred years ago this was the Empire State Building
and the Eiffel Tower and the Statue of Liberty all rolled into one,
and it still rivals each of those incredible buildings.

At the first corner I looked across the plaza to the Pyramid of
the Moon, lower, but still imposing. To me, now, it was a massive
embodiment of love. At the next corner, I looked out on a Mexican
village and across a huge plain to the mountains beyond. The third
corner was similar, and the last looked back down the Avenue of the
Dead. All around, across the vast plain, were mountains. Twice we
made this circuit, and every step was awesome.

"Wake up, old friends, wake up. It is time."

My voice spoke to the stones, as I walked around the terraces of
this Pyramid to the Sun. This was the culmination of a lifetime of
searching for a way to fill a lifelong emptiness. In Teo, I had come
to an acceptance that reached deeper and extended further than ever
before. After all the years of meetings and workshops, and everything
else that had been my path, I felt something different, the feeling I
had longed for. The realization was sweet; I had found the missing
part of me. Reaching the top of the Pyramid of the Sun, my awareness of two perceptions merged into one.

In the center, on top of the pyramid, Peggy sat facing us, as we made our way up the last few steps. Seeing Peggy was both a relief and a bit frightening. She sat in the lotus position with her eyes closed, and yet I had the very real feeling that she was looking at me. My attention was captivated by the space that surrounded her.

The breeze caressing my face felt alive. Peggy opened her eyes, motioning for me to come sit in front of her. Ted began placing the rest of our group in a circle surrounding us. My mind began to chatter away. *What are you doing? This is crazy, blah, blah, blah.*

Then Peggy said, "Let it go. Don't believe your head. Feel! Feel this place!"

Looking into her eyes, I felt the now familiar energy of the pyramid beneath me, the light of the sun passing through me. My body began to vibrate. I felt a very high-pitched resonance emitting from everything around me. The pyramid, Peggy, my body, everyone around us, even the earth and the sky, were vibrating faster and faster. I heard a hum, like the ones made by big power lines.

In the distance, as if he were in some other room, Ted spoke. "All life passes to earth through the sun. If the sun were to disappear, life on earth would cease to exist. The Creator feeds this world of form and light through the sun. This is our moment to open ourselves to the light and will of creation."

Suddenly a shock jolted my body. I was pushed down and back by energy passing through me. My eyes began to flutter. I felt Peggy's hand touch my forehead as lightning flashed across the darkness of my vision.

"Let go! Go into the light!"

Peggy guided me to an awareness that touched the Infinite. I felt my body as a conduit of energy, passing from the sun to the pyramid. My mind fought to retake control, but I was far beyond its ability to hook my attention. For a moment I felt like I might explode. One of the women sat down behind me. She put her arms tightly around me, trying to ground us to the earth. She alone was not enough, so Ted told another woman to do the same.

As we became grounded, I realized I was back in that place of color and light. I heard a hum. The sound had feeling; everything had feeling. The colors, the sounds, the light—all fed me the exquisite joy of pure love. I was back home, where I had come from before being Lee. There would never again be a doubt about the presence or nature of God. God is love. God is this, this moment, this awareness, this life. As I lay back against the woman behind me, Peggy touched my face and called me back. I did not want to let go. Slowly my awareness returned. I opened my eyes to see Ted's face wearing a giant knowing grin.

It was done.

My life had come full circle from arrival on planet Earth through forty years of living, to this timeless place of remembering. My prayers had been answered in a form that I didn't see coming, the only way they could have been answered. Ted helped me up from my seat on top of the Pyramid of the Sun. There were butterflies everywhere.

Looking out over the valley of Teotihuacán, I felt I was witnessing the potential of life on earth for the first time. I was at peace. I was in Love. I was home, in me, here.

After some photos and hugs, we descended the steps back to the Avenue of the Dead. Some of our group shifted back into shopper mode and headed out to spend their pesos. I felt found and lost at the same time. I had found what I'd been looking for, and I was at the same time so alone in this world of modern man. A small group of us headed to Ted and Peggy's favorite restaurant, La Gruta, the cave, which was literally in a huge cave, not far from the Pyramid of the Sun.

La Gruta descends about four stories into the ground, and the walls of the cave are lit with candles. There was a mariachi band and all the furniture was hand painted bright colors with tablecloths to match. After the intensity of the morning, settling into a seat in the cool atmosphere of La Gruta was just right. I remembered in the Carlos Castaneda books how don Juan told Carlos to drink a beer to help ground him, so I ordered a cold one and some chicken molé. It was funny to now use a cold beer to ground myself instead of drinking one to catch a buzz, but that is, in fact, exactly what I did. There was no need to talk, and still we laughed and chatted over the experiences of the day and the reality of our return home.

After chilling at La Gruta, we caught some local taxis, old Nissans with holes in the floorboard and saints and rosaries on the dash, and rode back to the hotel. I saw Dana sitting by the pool. As quick as I could, I changed into my swimsuit and went down to join her.

It is difficult to explain how just looking at her could shift my entire awareness. My experiences in Teo had connected me to a feeling within that filled my entire being. I knew the feeling was coming from within me, but looking at Dana seemed to magnify everything about it. Sitting by the pool, we talked about the connection we shared and how it was something beyond any experience we'd had before. To be able to look at someone and feel completely and totally in love and yet have no need to possess or act on the feeling amazed me.

Ted joined us, and I told him how I was feeling. He said, "What you're feeling is you. The truth is, what you feel is always you. We are taught to believe that it's the other person causing the feeling, and it's you all the time."

When I told him about the connection that Dana and I shared, he said simply, "You two have merged, two energies, two separate individuals; you merged like two rays of light coming together to make one."

I got it. That was a perfect explanation of how I felt. Looking around the courtyard and pool area, I was in love with everything—the birds, palm trees, water, people, life. I felt like I was surrounded by heaven on earth. As my mind wandered through the days in Teo to the coming journey home, I started laughing.

Dana looked at me. "Have you gone crazy?" she said.

"No, sweetie, I don't think I'm going crazy. I think I may be going sane." I couldn't stop laughing. Suddenly the serious business of life had lost its grip on me. "I know one thing. It's going to be interesting to go home tomorrow."

Our group gathered that evening and everyone shared their experiences of the day and all their love and gratitude for the entire journey.

Peggy gave us what she called "your reentry talk." She told us how we had opened our being to the energy and love that is Teotihuacán. We had lived in the last five days what two thousand years ago took years to experience. That was because the resonance, or vibration, of life on earth has increased in frequency many times over the last two thousand years.

"Your being here is literally an invitation from life to let go of living invested in suffering and fear, and your opportunity to choose from this day forward what you will create as your life on earth. There is no judgment or expectation with this invitation. It is simply now your choice. It is also now your responsibility, how you choose, what you choose. No one is doing anything to you anymore. It is you doing it to yourself."

We took in her words as she continued on, "You have had a magical experience here, and that's beautiful. Now it is up to you. Do you want freedom in your life? Are you willing to let go of all you think you know and examine every aspect of who and what you believe you are? This is where the real work starts, when you go home. If you are willing to give yourself one hundred percent of your love and attention, then you may want to apprentice with a teacher of this lineage. Someone who has walked their own path of transformation.

"Reclaiming our divinity, our truth, is the greatest gift we can give to life, to this world, to the one that created us. I want you to listen to this prayer of don Miguel's. Hear these words in your heart, as well as your mind:

"May 16th, 2001, the day of the Lord, when the divinity returns to us. When living our free will, and with all the power of our spirits we decide to live our lives in free communion with God, with no expectations. We will live our lives with gratitude, love, loyalty and justice, beginning with ourselves and continuing with our brothers and sisters. We will respect all creation as the symbol of our Love communion with the one who created us. To the eternal happiness of Humanity. Que tu sol sea brillante."

The tears came with such gratitude and sweetness that I couldn't speak. There was no need to speak. I had found my home, my peers, myself.

Peggy gave me a hug. "You did it," she said. "You'll be back."

Looking her in the eye, I said, "I'll never really leave here. This place is inside of me."

That night I dreamed a kaleidoscope of dreams, images of jaguars and eagles, of home and my daughters, of Teo thousands of years earlier. I woke up around five the next morning and lay in bed, feeling like every cell in my body was buzzing with light and life. I wasn't going back to sleep.

Lying there in bed I could smell the cattle from the ranch next to the hotel property. Memories of being a kid in bed at home on my dad's ranch in Wyoming flashed through my mind. I also thought about the beach in Florida, the taste of saltwater, and the smell of coconut oil. I tried to figure out how I would bring this experience to the Ranch and integrate it into what treatment and recovery could be about.

Just before sunrise the birds woke up, singing wide open. I got dressed and walked downstairs and out through the front of the villas to the road that runs around the Arqueological area. There was no one around as I stood at the fence looking down the Avenue of the Dead. Standing in the misty morning light at the other end of the Avenue was the Pyramid of the Moon. I wondered how the Spanish came to call this road of redemption the Avenue of the Dead. In that early morning light, it looked to me like the Avenue of Life.

In my heart I had a conversation with this magical place. I thanked the spirit of Quetzalcoatl for taking all that I had let go of on my journey. Closing my eyes I could see and smell the Temple of the Jaguars and the Palace of the Butterflies. I told the old one who had walked with me up the Pyramid of the Sun that I would be back, and I thanked all the masters who had come before for keeping this awareness alive for us.

To my right I heard the bawling of calves and the barking of the village dogs. As I turned, two cowboys rode out onto the street with a small bunch of sheep and cattle headed to a pasture down the road. I couldn't have felt more at home. Taking one last look down the avenue to the ancient city where "man awakens to God" I knew this was just the beginning.

Returning to the hotel I found our group having breakfast in the dining room. Between dreaming all night and getting up so early, I was *famished*. After breakfast we gathered in front of the hotel for some last-minute photos and said adios to the staff, who felt more like family now.

Loading the bus was a blur, and then we were gone, back to the world we'd left behind. Driving through Mexico City seemed like a slow-motion movie reel. The airport was a different story. The scene struck me as insane, like Stanley Kubrick meets Mexican soap opera.

Okay, man, just check in and then find somewhere to take a seat and watch this Showtime Original.

After checking in I saw Dana standing in the security line. That intense feeling still had life. The *federales* checked our passports, and we proceeded to the international concourse. I was trying to decide how I might convince her to come back to Tennessee with me, knowing all the time that wasn't what our connection was about. I still had to try. Dana was as sweet and solid as always. She smiled and shook her head. "You know that's not happening, sweet man," she said.

We hugged and kissed good-bye ten times like we were high school sweethearts, until I almost missed my flight. From the air, I looked out across the landscape of Mexico—from the volcanic mountain peaks to the chaos of the city below—and I wondered how this place would fit into my life in the future.

There was no doubt that my relationship with Mexico had just begun. Hell, my relationship with myself had just begun.

CHAPTER 17

The Spiritual Connection Within

One plane change and seven hours later, I walked off the aircraft at Nashville International Airport, and, although everything was familiar, nothing was the same. The air was thick and humid, middle Tennessee in early summer. I drove home buzzing with the energy of Teo in my veins.

I called my youngest daughter and told her I'd come pick her up after school the next day. I missed my girls. It was nine at night and I was hungry, so I hit a fast-food drive-thru, being reindoctrinated into Gringolandia.

I drove home to the ranch in silence, listening to the whine of the tires and the wind through the open window. The next morning was a repeat of my last morning in Mexico. I woke up at 5:00 AM and had to get out of bed and make coffee. As the sun rose, I poured another mug and headed out to see the cattle and horses. The land was home to me. Whenever I'd been gone from the ranch for a while, I'd crave getting out on the land to idle along and take a look. My dad and A.D. used to do the same thing when I was a kid, and I never knew why until I found myself repeating this tradition.

I needed to breathe the place in and see everything through the clarity of my Teo vision. "Teo vision," that's funny and it's the truth. I felt so peaceful. This was the feeling I'd only had glimpses of before my trip to Mexico. Treatment had given me inspiration and opportunity, but I had never really felt the depth of peace that I found in Teotihuacán.

After covering the home ranch, I drove the three miles to Pinewood Farm, the home of our second ranch, and stopped in at the Pinewood store to grab a country-ham biscuit. The Pinewood Ranch housed the offices of the Ranch Treatment Center, and I was ready to have a conversation with Sam, our program director.

Sam was a Vietnam vet who had lived his experience in hell. He was the kind of guy I'd want on my side when the trouble starts. We had spent hours talking about life and recovery and what really matters. I appreciated him most for his absolute dedication to the clients and their right to go as far as they chose for themselves. We also shared the fact that we didn't believe the world's story of itself. Some would say we were both the same kind of crazy. Whatever! We cared about the people we worked with.

"So, how was Mexico?" Sam was looking at me like he saw the energy rushing through my veins.

"It was a trip, amazing. I don't know, man, but what we've been calling recovery is getting ready to change, if I have anything to do with it."

Sam grinned, one of his "Okay! Oh well, here we go" kind of grins.

We talked for an hour. I told him he had to go himself. In fact, everyone on the staff had to go. No expectations—just check it out. My business partner thought I'd lost it. She's a sincere Southern Baptist and my newfound point of view was too much for her. When she asked if I'd joined a cult, I said, "No. In fact, I think what I've found is the antidote for cults, and, to tell you the truth, this world is looking like one big cult." That was the beginning of our going in two very different directions. She was headed toward more tradition and religion, and I was going toward the Sun and Stars.

The next day I called Ted and Peggy and told them, "I want to go for it, for the freedom Peggy spoke of. Whatever that takes, I'm game." I wanted to continue working with them as my teachers.

Ted laughed, "I told Peggy you'd call. So you're ready to die to the life you've been living?"

"Yeah. I have no doubts," I replied with true conviction.

✦   ✦   ✦

Dana and I stayed in touch, talking once or twice a week. She also apprenticed with Peggy. I invited her to visit the Ranch and experience some of the work that we did. She brought her sister for a family equine weekend workshop in September. It was sweet to see her. That impulse of wanting her as a lover had passed, but the deeper, true connection of spirits had not at all.

I incorporated *The Four Agreements* by don Miguel Ruiz, which started my adventure in Mexico, into the program at the Ranch. Because one of our primary therapists was already using it with the clients, we made it an official part of the program. When clients checked into the Ranch, not only did they get *The Big Book*, but they also got *The Four Agreements*. Of course there were reactions from some of the traditional 12-Step people to adding "nonrecovery reading" to a treatment program. We did it anyway. We started a weekly meeting on *The Four Agreements*, which meant one less 12-Step meeting. This bordered on blasphemy, but this wasn't a 12-Step meeting; it was treatment. We were respectful of the program, and we weren't trying to sell it.

Some clients loved this new perspective and some wanted to resist anything that wasn't what they had been taught before coming to the Ranch, which was do what you're told and you'll be okay. Do what you're told and you're not responsible. This can undermine personal transformation. *The Four Agreements* offered a path to reclaim our unique expression in life. This was a path of awareness, not rules of freedom, not compliance. Through taking 100-percent personal responsibility for our lives, we reclaim the energy and power to create our life from integrity, free from the past as our identity—a real step to happy, joyous, and free.

We were waking up to the truth that had been within us all along. We had to if we were going to undo our greatest addiction—the addiction to fear and suffering. All the tools of the recovery world, the religious world, and the self-help world were just that: tools. No matter how good a tool is, the tool is *never* responsible for the hand that guides it.

I asked Ted and Peggy if they would come to the Ranch and lead a workshop on the basics of the Toltec teachings. They agreed, so we set a November date. Again, many recovery people and professionals asked me, "What does any of that have to do with recovery?" Of course the answer to their question would depend on what one's definition of "recovery" was, and mine was wide open.

Challenging that perception was tricky in a world where fear is the baseline for decision. Fear will never lead to freedom. "Happy, joyous, and free" is not the same today as it will be next month or next year. Any mirror of how we create our own suffering is a gift on the journey to freedom. Fear has an insatiable appetite that demands we feed it our attention and faith. To live with fear as a guide is to live in hell, and that is what we're recovering from, not to. The way out of fear is reclaiming faith in ourselves.

That might sound blasphemous to many, but if you don't connect to Spirit within, you are always taking someone else's word for things. It's a dependency. Life is too important to lean on someone else's interpretation of the truth rather than finding your own. Recovery is about finding that spiritual connection within.

That November Ted and Peggy came to the Ranch, and Dana, her sister, and an eclectic group of friends showed up for the first Toltec Recovery workshop. The weekend was a great success. There were all kinds of questions and reactions as well as subtle awakenings and brilliant "aha's." We re-created some of the processes I had experienced in Teotihuacán—opening to possibilities, looking at out attachments, and how we were so defined by our stories.

Ted and Peggy brought a friend with them, Meaghan (Mee), who turned out to be the sweetest gift in my life since my daughter Ana was born fifteen years before. We spent that weekend together, and, when she left, she invited me to visit her in L.A. I went, and, once again, what I called reality was rocked into hyperspace. Mee and I had been talking by phone for a month before she came. Ted had introduced us, as we both had a lot of common interests in Shamanic world adventures. There was no romantic energy between Dana and me, and there was a great relationship of soul-to-soul respect and appreciation. Mee, on the other hand, had a big red heart flashing right overhead.

Mee is now my wife, and we have two amazing daughters. We have lived between our ranches in Tennessee, the beach in Malibu, and our magical Mexico. My life is bigger, brighter, and more grounded than I could have ever imagined. I still surf, cowboy, lead journeys to Sacred places, and play with my girls.

✦ ✦ ✦

From Lee Today, 2013

To sum up the rest of it, we sold the Ranch Recovery business in 2010. It was time for my business partner and me to part ways. We did a lot of great things together, but life had called us in different directions. I am still the landlord for the Ranch Treatment Program, as this land is my place of deep-grounded connection; in fact, it is the foundation for the integrity of the treatment center. We recently opened an outpatient program called the Integrative Life Center (ILC) in Nashville. As I learn and grow, my perspective on healing and recovery expands. ILC is the next incarnation of healing and solid recovery opportunities. It is a living dream of love and transformation. We are organic farming out on the Pinewood Farm, and Piney River Cattle Company has become a grass-fed beef, lamb, and hog operation—all natural, all the time.

My dreaming continues. I am determined to create a retreat center for veterans and their families, which is another huge need that is not being addressed in our culture. I now have a home in Teotihuacán, and I spend two or three months a year in that magical place introducing groups to the mysteries of the pyramids. I call these trips Spirit Recovery Journeys (spiritrecovery.com).

The Toltecs of ancient Mexico saw our lives as living dreams that we create either with or without awareness. Awareness is the key to mastering our relationship with life. By healing my trespasses against myself, I have been freed of the need to live up to the expectations of the world. I have also freed the world from responsibility for my happiness.

The Second Coming is within you—it's an awakening, a rebirth into the spirit. With each thought and action, we each choose the experiences of our life on earth. Look in that mirror and be honest. Are you dreaming heaven on earth or something else?

These days I no longer think of myself as "in recovery."

I am recovered. Today, I'm in life, and I'm in love with that life.

May peace be with you.

Part Two

FILLING YOUR MEDICINE BAG

In this part, you'll uncover three major themes. The first is *conscious connection*. Conscious connection is you being grounded, centered, and present in your body and in touch with your innate sacredness. From there, you connect with the signals being sent from Spirit that will lead you home—you, on the Mother Ship, seatbelt buckled! The next theme explores the power of imagination. This is about uncovering your hopes and dreams and being connected to the spiritual power to make them come true. The third theme is transformation—opening up to the endless opportunities in life and allowing them to become real . . . or you being happy, joyous, and free.

The ideas and practices suggested for your medicine bag are directed toward building and strengthening these three basic principles. They do not always work in a linear way. This book sets the stage and assists you in getting the conversation started, but it's your movie. You may wish to read this book straight through or skim through it to see what speaks to you the loudest. Read those parts first and come back to the others later. It's your call.

These pages contain medicine from a variety of sources. You'll find concepts from traditional psychology, Native American wisdom, ancient Vedic teachings, 12-Step stories, quantum spirituality, and the folk wisdom of the ages. The exercises we've included have been thoroughly road tested and have helped many recovering folks break through limited thinking and living and transform themselves and their lives.

You can work through the medicine bag on your own, but the practices really come alive in a group. This is because healing is synergistic, meaning it is more than the sum of its parts. There's power in working together and much to learn from each other.

Many Roads, Many Travelers

Healing begins in your heartfelt *desire* for life along with a firm *intention* to walk toward the light and the *commitment* to follow that impulse. Regardless of whether you are on a 12-Step path, pursuing individual counseling, still looking for your path, or toughing it out on your own, what is being offered here builds on whatever you have accomplished. It doesn't replace it.

The healing journey begins as you let go of whatever is in the way of allowing it to happen. This means different things to different people. If you have struggled with substance abuse, it means letting it go. If you are coping with self-negating behaviors, it means letting them go. If you want to be in your life in a new way, it means letting go of the old way and being willing to be new.

Are you willing to let go of those things that have held you back and kept you prisoner so that you can move forward on your journey toward wholeness and happiness? If so, simply turn the page and begin the adventure your spirit has been urging you to take.

CHAPTER 18

Awakening Consciousness

"In the transformational process, we
become artists and scientists of our own lives.
In the transformational life, our perceptions are changed.
We become whole seeing and creative.
We become playful and recapture the childlike
qualities of being human.
We let go of our denial and rigidity and open to flow."

—Marilyn Ferguson (1938–),
American author, editor, speaker

C ontemporary culture tosses around the term *transformation* quite freely. Think of the world of advertising: A new coat of paint can *transform* your house, a garden is *transformed* by a makeover, the right shampoo has the potential to *transform* your life, and so on. Each of these examples is about superficial change. Transformation goes much deeper than the surface. Transformation is the process of waking up; it's about your coming to awareness of who you are and what you are about in your heart and soul. Transformation permeates your entire being—body, mind, spirit, hopes, dreams, and memories—and it carries the raw potential to create a future that reflects your truth.

Organic to our physiological, psychological, and spiritual nature, transformation opens the pathway to your authenticity and to living the awareness of the miracle that is you.

In a nutshell, transformation is about growing up spiritually. It takes the opportunity you have given yourself in recovery and runs with it, leading you toward wholeness.

We often begin this journey by taking a look around outside ourselves. When we fail to find our answers "out there," we might look inside as a last-ditch effort. When we do look inside, we have the chance to step into ourselves at the soul level. We can anchor our lifeline in this holy ground and follow the dream that is written on our hearts. Such opportunities are steeped in grace—a favor from God that influences our choices.

Choice is paramount here. Grace is a gift freely given—no strings attached. You can say no to grace. You can make the decision to stay in your comfort zone even when it isn't comfortable anymore. Or you can say yes to your dream, not knowing exactly what it will ask of you or where it will take you. There's mystery in transformation.

*There was a sense of freedom in knowing how broken down I was. It
was actually a relief. I had left behind miserable relationships, lawsuits,
nightmares, and broken hearts. Expect a miracle? You bet! If it's miracles
you're offering, I could sure use one.*

—From Lee's Story

In our transformed consciousness, we see ourselves differently
from the level of imagination and purpose to the manifestation of
our deep hopes and dreams. It implies changing for the better; we
don't transform down. In her book *Paradoxology: Spirituality in a
Quantum Universe,* Miriam Therese Winter describes transformation
as a conversion experience, where our mind and our life are radically
and substantially changed—a change that goes beyond change.

This *"change beyond change"* is an awakening of spirit—a growing
awareness of feelings and perceptions and possibilities that were once
beyond our ability to grasp. In recovery, people talk about suddenly
seeing the beauty of their surroundings. The grass appears greener,
the sky seems bluer, the birds chirp a little louder, and they feel a
sense of euphoria. Once awakened, awareness continues growing and
changing your sense of yourself and your relationship to life—with
your permission and a little prompting.

In our metamorphosed consciousness, we catch a glimpse of our
beauty and our potential to be a positive influence in the world. Looking at ourselves through heightened awareness, we are able to see our
patterns—both the ones that are still serving us, and those holding
us captive in our old skin. We are emboldened to challenge limiting
beliefs and empowered to push into new territory. Led by curiosity
and inspired by imagination, we are guided to our own authenticity by
instincts and impulses installed by our creator—a virtual GPS calling
us home to ourselves. Stepping into the role of co-creators that we
were born to be, we are no longer lulled into desperation and despair

or driven by anxiety, but we see a field of infinite possibilities and are given to activating these gifts.

Butterflies Are Us

Nearly everyone is familiar with the life cycle of the butterfly: the egg is laid, the caterpillar hatches and begins to eat, the chrysalis is formed, and then finally a butterfly emerges and immediately goes about its life's work of mating and carrying pollen from plant to plant. In this ongoing cycle, more eggs are laid, more caterpillars hatch, more chrysa-lises are formed, and more butterflies emerge. In this way, life in the meadow flourishes. Like the butterfly, we are genetically programmed to move from an insular need for security in the necessary chrysalis of childhood to our emergence into a larger field of possibilities as we dry our wings in the sunlight and take flight so that life itself may flourish.

So the cowboy went into treatment. I got bled, weighed, and medicated. I was interviewed, assessed, and assigned. At some point during those first few days, I was told that if I could surrender—if I would let go and let God—I could learn to live happy, joyous, and free.

—From Lee's Story

The Journey Toward Consciousness

Like all spiritual truths, transformation is paradoxical—it begins with an ending. The world, as you know it, starts coming undone. A new pattern is being woven, but you don't realize that when you're standing hip deep in the shreds of the old one. Fear of uncertainty is universal, and stepping into the mystery is scary. Transformation demands new levels of faith—lots of it. Faith will provide a hesitant heart the needed boost to get over, under, or around those internal walls and onto the freedom trail. Faith brings an end to limiting beliefs and outgrown attitudes that are no longer needed *if* you're willing to surrender them—and sometimes whether you're willing or not.

Being human is a work in progress. Millions of cells die each day and new ones are created in an ongoing process throughout life. These cells carry consciousness—our story as we have lived it. According to Deepak Chopra, endocrinologist and leader in mind-body healing, cells in the body regenerate with what he calls "phantom memory," each generation of cells patterning the next generation. These new cells will be exact replicas of the ones that precede them—unless the program is changed.

In tens of thousands of case studies of survivors who had healed emotional, physical, and spiritual injuries, Chopra's research discovered two common factors: first was the survivor's recognition of the body's innate intelligence, awareness of its connection to "Spirit" or "Source"; second was the ability to emotionally resolve the trauma—to *let it go.* When these two conditions were present, the cells *returned* to their original healthy state. There was no further passing on of the trauma and the new cells were born healthy. Your new story is waiting to be written informed by awakened consciousness.

It is human nature to balk at change, and, at the same time, like caterpillars, we are drawn toward our own awakening. We see possibilities and our resolve strengthens, and we become willing to clear any obstacles in our way to fully attaining it. We call this process of awakening consciousness *dreaming*—because it is as if we awaken from an old dream and step into a new way of seeing reality.

An Inspired Dream

We are born with a dream in our heart and the capacity to create our lives out of this dream—if the process isn't derailed. Dreams aren't solid. They are ideas, impulses, or potential asking to be realized. Dreams are shaped by culture—family, society, religion, economics and education, genetics, where we live, and whom we know. These powerful influences can help us manifest our dream or they can overpower it with their agendas, driving it underground—but they can't annihilate it. Consciousness gives us the opportunity to rediscover a forgotten dream and the possibility of making it come true.

> *As my interview came to a close she said, "The journey you're embarking on isn't easy, but you're worth it, so hang in there."*
>
> *I thanked her and said, "I just want to be happy—happy, joyous, and free. . . ."*
>
> *I walked out of her office feeling like there was hope. I was told a lot of stuff and given all kinds of information, but nothing stuck with me as much as "happy, joyous, and free."*
>
> —From Lee's Story

A new dream often begins with an "aha!" moment—a sudden flash of insight shakes us up and wakes us up. In that moment of awakening, hope is born. We catch sight of a different reality, and we realize there is a way out of whatever trap we've found ourselves in. Such a transforming moment is exhilarating; it *awakens* a sense of possibility, and it points us in a new direction. As electrifying as it may be, lasting change doesn't happen in a moment. On our own and without a practice to sustain us, it's hard to hold on to a dream long enough for it to take root. Like any growing thing, consciousness needs *tending*.

Fellow Sojourners on Common Ground

Many people have experienced the transformative power of *tending* by following a spiritual practice. Repetition takes a flash of insight and grounds it in the skin and bones of reality—literally, down into the marrow of our bones where our new cells are made with new awareness. Birthing and nurturing our emerging self needs the encouragement of community—ideally a community of people who have likewise said yes to life.

We invite you to step into the circle and join with likehearted folks who are walking many different paths together. This may be your treatment group or your recovery group or a group of people you pull together to go through the exercises in this book—fellow sojourners. As you become rooted in your own process, you gain respect for others' beliefs and find them interesting rather than threatening. You see them as the great diversity of Spirit's expression—God's crazy quilt!

I didn't have to agree with everything to get what I needed in the moment. The answer was in my willingness to accept help. I wasn't completely through trying to figure everything out, and, at the same time, I could see I needed some help. My shell of personal importance cracked. Maybe I didn't have all the answers. Maybe I could stand to learn a thing or two about life.

—From Lee's Story

Ultimate Reality and Our Human Relationship

As Richard W. Clark, author of *Addictions & Spiritual Transformation*, says, "Our bodies are the temples within which the essence of God resides. Contact with the soul or the spirit begins through and within our own physical being." This is in tune with a Hindu belief that states "Atman is Brahman." This is part of a complex ancient teaching that describes Ultimate Reality and our human relationship to it.

Roughly translated, "Atman" is our individual soul—the essence of each living thing. People, animals, plants—everything has soul, or Atman. Atman is eternal and exists within the body, which is mortal. "Brahman" refers to cosmic soul—*the eternal essence of the universe and the ultimate Divine reality*. It is Source and Creator of all. Our individual soul and the Universal Soul (God) are one. Our soul is of the same substance as the Cosmic or Universal Soul. Contact with our soul happens through and within our own physical being.

It doesn't matter if you have disconnected from your body in an attempt to escape intolerable circumstances or have overidentified with your body by denying your spiritual nature. Either way, the pathway to healing and growth is the same. Establishing respectful communication with your body, nurturing it, getting the static off the mental wires, and opening the lines of communication with Spirit is the agenda. Failing to respect your body as the physical form of the Sacred has created chaos on a massive scale. Transformation increases your desire for healing as your consciousness expands to embrace your divine nature, and it decreases the possibility of settling for less.

Our mind wants to make spirituality more complicated than simply going outside and sitting on the ground, but our sacred stories indicate that it can be that simple—*definitely not easy*, but simple. Jesus, an earthly emissary of the Divine, was born in a stable and lived his life walking dusty back roads with his simple message to "Love one another." His students sat on riverbanks. White Buffalo Woman brought the sacred ceremonies to the Lakota people appearing in the spirit of the Buffalo. Siddhartha Gautama, the spiritual teacher later known as the Buddha, found enlightenment, realizing his divine nature while sitting on the ground under the Bodhi tree.

While millions and millions of books have been written about these stories, the events themselves were quite straightforward. It is our inability to accept our divine nature that complicates everything. So says the English anthropologist Gregory Bateson: "The major problems with the world are the result of the difference between how nature works and the way people think." Awakening our consciousness brings us into alignment with nature.

The following is our list of common characteristics or ways of being that nurture the process of awakening consciousness. We encourage you to add your own ideas to this list.

- Choose to celebrate life, value consciousness, and be alert.
- Be authentically you; resist conformity for the sake of conformity and rebellion for the sake of rebellion.
- Connect with the joy of your inner child and the wisdom of your higher self.
- Question your core beliefs and find your truth.
- Maintain a sustainable lifestyle, balancing body, mind, and spirit.
- Seek higher meaning and purpose.
- Feed your expanding vision by exploring ideas, art, music, and the sacred writings of many traditions.

Walk the spiritual path of your choosing.

Buckle Yourself In!

Awareness of the physical indwelling of spirit lies at the heart and soul of healing and growth. While people seem to emphasize the "God" side of spiritual connection, that side is in good shape. It is our end of the cord that gets unplugged! The goal of Spirit Recovery is to help you get your spirit connected to your body, your mind clear of other people's stuff, and emotionally present in the here and now. That's where it all happens—life, hopes, dreams . . . reality. Everyone gets to define for him or herself what "success" means on this journey. Our idea includes feeling reasonably comfortable and safe in the world, engaging life, and following our impulse to transform and live authentically.

Being grounded in our body is primary. That's where life is lived and that is where we experience our connection with Spirit. What our fellow travelers have taught us over the years is that grounding happens best when we are consciously connected to the *Mother Ship*—the little green planet we live on.

Nature doesn't lie, it doesn't try to con you, it doesn't need anything from you, and it has no investment in what you say or believe; it simply is. Likewise, we can't con nature. Nature's radical honesty is transforming. It awakens our longing for truth—our desire for authenticity. We are of the earth; she is our chicken soup. Earth consciousness is good medicine.

The spiritual journey is about wholeness—finding our truth and living it. While we may all have a different picture over our head when the topic of God comes up, *earth* is a solid and living representation of what can only be symbolized. Earth unifies and sustains us. Earth is home base regardless of where you worship, how you vote, where you grocery shop, or what kind of a car you drive. We are traveling through space on this little green ship together—a package deal. Your physical body is your seat on the Mother Ship. Isolation and fear dissolve in our awakened sense of belonging; we are returned to original knowledge of *wholeness*. We do that best when we are connected to earth—"she" is the healer.

INSIDE THE MEDICINE BAG:
Tools for Awakening Consciousness

Asking yourself thought-provoking questions brings your subconscious closer to the surface, thereby helping you to discover your personal truth. So, ask yourself the following questions, being sure to dig really deep to locate the most honest answers you can find. If you have a journal, feel free to journal your responses. If you are part of a group, consider sharing.

- What words or ideas caught your attention as you read this chapter? How did they feel to you?
- If transformation is about growing up spirituality, how old do you feel?
- What do you imagine it would feel like to step into your soul?
- What is the story you tell yourself that keeps you from being you? How does that story make you feel?
- Grace is a divinely inspired opportunity. When have you said no to grace? How did that feel?
- When have you said yes to grace? How did that feel?
- What is your hope as you begin this part of your transformational journey?
- How does hope feel?
- What are your fears?
- How would you feel if you had no fear?
- Are you ready to write a new story, create a new dream for yourself?

CHAPTER 19

Searching for Self-Understanding

"A spiritually optimistic point of view holds that the universe is woven out of a fabric of love. Everything that is happening is ultimately for the good if we're willing to face it head-on and use our adversities for soul growth."

—Joan Borysenko (1945–), psychologist, author, mind/body integration pioneer

Transformation stands you on new ground, but before you can get there, it's helpful to know the ground on which you stand and a bit about how you got here. We use the term *matrix* to identify the web of unspoken assumptions and beliefs on which a culture is built. As a member of the matrix, it is largely your reality, although you may not be aware of how it impacts you. The matrix functions at the subconscious level until you take the time to examine it, which most of us don't do. We call it the cultural *dream* because, like a dream, it is only as real as our belief in it. The matrix is a work in progress, always evolving into the next "next thing." And there are tipping points—swing moments when the changes that have been gathering energy below the surface break into consciousness. Many people believe we are currently at a collective tipping point in this inevitable shift.

> *To unravel our lives, we must begin at the beginning. We have to work our way into our core and back out again. In our core, we keep our deepest, most sacred beliefs and agreements. Some of those are so old and are buried so deep that we've lost awareness of them. They have become secrets we keep from ourselves.*
>
> —From Lee's Story

In exploring the matrix, it's important to know that not everyone within it agrees with the assumptions. This is particularly true of Native American cultures, many other non-Western cultures, and a growing number of "just plain others." However, the present systems and structures of society are formed in the matrix described in this chapter, and most folks are living with the matrix assumptions. We'll begin with a lightning-quick trip through the evolution of thought in Western culture, using a fast-moving time machine and a very broad brush! So, fasten your seat belts as we zip back 50,000 years or more to see how our earliest ancestors might have experienced reality. Interestingly, remnants of this ancient worldview are still with us today. As you read through this chapter notice what is true for you. This information can help you clear up some of the mystery as well as spark a new insight.

When Magic Met Reason

We are "meaning makers," and we need to make sense out of our world. We do this to create order out of chaos, to experience coherence and purpose—and because it is human instinct. Our ageless search for self-understanding began long ago, at the dawn of the human story, as our earliest ancestors created meaning by painting images on cave walls. The images indicate that a mother figure was central to society, and rituals and ceremonies celebrating her were common.

Archaeological findings show that these early cultures revolved around the seasons and the movements of the sun, moon, and stars. Our ancestors chanted, drummed, and danced, honoring what is depicted as a seamless relationship between nature and the sacred. They personalized nature, understanding cosmic forces in terms of human emotion and human action. Goddesses and gods were assigned realms over which they ruled. They threw lightning bolts when they were angry, commanded the seas, coaxed the seeds out of the earth, swallowed the sun at night, and pulled the moon across the sky by chariot. Maintaining these relationships—between the gods and earth and the gods and humans—assured our ancestors' survival.

In this poetic understanding, when something went wrong—when the river threatened to sweep the village away or when the mountain breathed fire—something had to be done. We developed rituals and ceremonies to please and appease the deities. Our Judeo/Christian/Islamic roots grew out of these stories, which reach back in time and place, connecting us through our common origins. Eons ago, we sat around fires and painted our stories on the rocks—we drank out of the same wells. While we think we have grown past these stories, they continue to carry deep meaning; they have the power to unite us and can also drive us to war.

Our ancestors were hunter-gatherers, and the Great Mother was considered present in the earth—she provided for her children and she was honored. Art, agriculture, and metallurgy developed as well as the use of herbs and herbal medicine. Crops were planted, animals were domesticated, and commerce began. Moving from matriarchal to patriarchal culture in the Western world spanned many thousands of years, during which our relationship with the Great Mother gradually changed, as did our relationship with the earth and with our own physical existence.

Our understanding of the Sacred was taking on an otherworldly character; eventually it would shift completely from female to male and from the experience of the Sacred in nature (including us) to confining it to the heavenly realm. In removing the creator from creation, we began to distrust our own experiences—intuition and even instinct were disregarded.

The Age of Reason

Out of the poetic world, and perhaps in response to it, sometime around the 1500s and 1600s, the left hemisphere of our brain awakened and rational thought emerged as a force to be reckoned with. Science and mathematics replaced poetry and song, and we began to think of ourselves as separate from nature—above it and smarter. Our relationship with nature changed from one based on respect and reciprocity to one based on dominance. We broke natural law and asserted our rights over nature.

The left hemisphere is our get-real brain. It is literal, rather than symbolic. This left-brain preference became the defining characteristic of Western culture; we valued analytical reasoning over sensing, feeling, or emotion, disconnecting us from our instinct and intuition, and our relational consciousness suffered a blow. Our reasoning mind sees how things are different, rather than how they are alike, and it creates categories as a way of understanding.

During the Age of Reason, we mapped the natural world, defining each individual piece of it down to the subatomic particles and beyond. We placed nature into Kingdoms, Phyla, Classes, Orders, Families, Genera, and Species based on how each was different from its neighbor. We defined the periodic table of elements, naming every substance we could find. We underwent an industrial revolution, as well as several other revolutions; we went to the moon and back and landed a spacecraft on Mars. Science, industry, and technology all took giant steps forward. We mapped the human genome; science reigned, and the sacred was evicted from nature and given a new address.

Having no way of rationally understanding the numinous aspect of existence, we placed "it" outside the material world—outside of creation. In doing that, we separated ourselves from our gods and our body from our soul. In this new compartmentalized arrangement, religion and science squared off; each ruled a realm of existence. Religion took the poetic position—believing in things we can't see or weigh or measure—and science took a material one. The two realms seemed to be in opposition to each other. Religion eventually fell under the spell of reason, and we struggled to understand concretely what could only be known intuitively and instinctively. Our innate sense of the sacred—an *experience* or a *feeling* rather than a mathematical equation—was discounted, and the mind ruled.

Elaborate theology was developed in hopes of creating a rationale that could explain the sacred; we believed that, given the right logic, we could prove the existence of God once and for all. Human experiences—holding a sleeping baby, standing in awe of a mountain, or witnessing a breathtaking sunset—weren't good enough. We had to have *proof* of the sacred. Try as we did, the intrinsic unity of spirit and matter would not roll over for science—it would not go away.

Science, based in our left brain, couldn't fully grasp the right brain's relational sensibility. The power that's packed into that "empty" space between things remained a mystery, a burr under the saddle of science.

Quantum Consciousness: Dreaming Wholeness

Fast-forward to the dawn of the last century when mathematics and physics rocked the world with their discovery of the quantum field—the vitally alive substance that permeates everything from mountain to molecule, and within which everything exists. Quantum reality breaks the old rules of both science and religion; it shows how we exist as both wave (spirit) and particle (body) at the same time, how we can be in more than one place at one time, and how there is no time!

In this enlivened quantum matrix, the ancient mythopoetic understanding of the world comes toe to toe with science—not to continue the battle, but to embrace one another. Our new dream is rooted in new physics, where mathematical equations show us—in terms we can believe—that it's all connected and it's all happening now!

Religion and science merge in this vibrant new understanding. Quantum consciousness explores each tiny speck of creation down to the very atoms of life and further into invisible "stuff" called quanta, while at the same time understanding wholeness and the web of life in which everything exists. This radical new science is the science of relationship—and it begins inside as we find ourselves and mend the sacred relationship between our body and soul.

Quantum theory is still downloading into the culture and integrating into the structures and systems of society. Remember, the last major shift took thousands of years. That was before cell phones, the Internet, and Ferraris. This time it will be much faster. In the meantime, we still live and do business in the old model. The matrix in which we live is built on separation, while our personal reality is already shifting or has already shifted to understanding wholeness and the presence of spirit everywhere. Our challenge is to live life on life's terms in this interesting and confusing time, without lapsing into denial or believing we're crazy—or that everyone else is!

Existing and Emerging Assumptions Inside the Matrix

Every culture has a variety of dreams as well as dreamers and also a prevailing dream that shapes reality for everyone. It's our *groupthink*— our family-of-origin story on a grand scale. Like our family story, a lot goes on below the surface that feels weird and isn't talked about. This is not necessarily for negative reasons, but because it's assumed that everyone's on board—that everyone has the same hopes and dreams and the same chance of bringing those dreams into reality.

It takes considerable time and energy to figure out a cultural matrix. You've grown up with it and probably aren't aware of how it influences your life. It seems like reality. At the same time, having perceptions different from the mainstream, as many of us do, can feel like we're up against something we can't quite see. Like the invisible dog fence, it can stop us in our tracks.

We're not talking about the everyday differences that we all have about anything from which team will win the World Series to who'll be the next president. We are talking about disagreement based on different realities. Identifying the core assumptions of culture creates clarity and gives us a firmer platform for forming our own philosophy of life, a necessary step in claiming our authenticity. The following are some examples of the shifting matrix assumptions compared with the emerging ones. You can assess where you are in the transformation process and possibly gain more self-understanding.

Accepting and believing that fitting in the established order in my life set me up on a foundation of lies. From that point on I was no longer authentic. From that point forward I sought from the world the validation that I was good enough. Accepting the world's perception of what I would be if I were good enough required that I reject myself.

—From Lee's Story

Compartmentalized Toward Holistic

The existing matrix in our Western society is compartmentalized; it is built on separation. It sees how things are different. It separates human beings from the rest of nature and sees "us" and "it" as opposing forces. It further divides human beings into body, mind, and spirit as distinct and independent parts of one another. It separates our sense of spirituality from the everyday affairs of the world, making it about the next life, not this one. It is overly dependent on logic—separating us from our feelings and our natural empathy.

The emerging matrix is holistic. It is *relational,* seeing how things connect rather than how they are separate. It sees humans as inter-related systems of body, mind, and spirit in relationship with self, with each other, and with the rest of the natural world. Holism respects law and order but leans toward spiritual principles such as justice and fair play in decision-making. It understands that situations and circumstances matter to people's lives. It lives from the whole brain—understanding logic and human empathy as two parts of a powerful system. It knows that logic separated from empathy is not really logical.

Where are you on the following scale? In which direction are you moving?

Compartmental <————————————> **Holistic**

Absolutism Toward Relativity

The existing matrix is based in absolutism—it sees things as either black or white, either one way or the other, either right or wrong with no middle ground. And it perceives humankind in a battle between good and evil. There isn't much room for mistakes, and the price of making one is high (think heaven or hell)—for eternity, no escape.

Holism is *relative,* meaning it sees opposites in relation to each other. Holism understands that humans have the capacity to be both good and bad, both creative and destructive—at any given time; it all depends on where we focus our energy. Holism is much less likely to invoke the categories of good and evil, but might look at whether a given decision has a positive or negative result—it looks at right or wrong relative to circumstances rather than as absolutes.

Where are you on the following scale? In which direction are you moving?

Absolutism <————————————> **Relativity**

Power over Toward Power Within

The existing matrix sees power as something you acquire from external sources and believes that power is a limited commodity. It therefore creates separation and competition as it strives to gain *power over* others by material one-upsmanship—a bigger house, more money, a higher position on the corporate ladder, a better education, more fame, or beauty—or whatever is being upheld by society. A power over paradigm is a top-down model and is based in dominance, believing that those on the top have more power, meaning privilege, over those below—and that this is a God-given reality.

In spiritual terms, this model is likely to relate to God as a symbol of power and might, rather than God as a symbol of love and caring. It tends to equate the acquisition of worldly power with gaining God's favor. In theory, it tends to believe that poverty and misfortune are signs of immorality rather than social or cultural issues primarily caused by limited opportunity. Power over does not necessarily believe that it owes anything back to society.

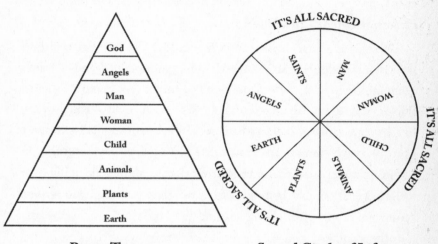

**Power Tower:
Power Over**

**Sacred Circle of Life:
Power Within**

Power within understands power as sacred presence in us and in creation. It believes everyone has the same amount of power and deserves the same consideration and respect. It is a spiritual model rather than a materialistic one. It extends this sense of indwelling creator to all creatures and all of nature. Power within is a partnership model. It is communal, seeing people working together to create social conditions that are favorable to all, including the sustainable use of resources. Power within understands that we have different gifts and talents but believes all are deserving of equal respect and access to opportunity. Power over might relate to helping others as a *handout*.

Power within would relate to helping others as offering a *hand up*. The power within model holds a social responsibility to build a more just world based on equality as a moral mandate.

Where are you on the following scale? In which direction are you moving?

Power Over <————————————> Power Within

External Toward Internal

The existing matrix is *externally* focused. We excel at building skyscrapers and rocket ships and becoming millionaires, and we value occupations that fit into those kinds of material accomplishments. Pursuits that aren't valued by culture are often ridiculed. ("You're going to do *what?* Lots of luck with *that!*") What aspiring artist has not heard some version of "You can't make money drawing pictures"? As a culture, we have a preference for cognitive/analytical thinking over feeling, intuition, and instinct, which we are often taught to ignore. However, feelings create human connection, and that's where empathy for others comes from. Awareness of higher values such as creativity, love, justice, fairness, and compassion is located in our feeling side, giving us the impetus to be of service.

Our current matrix bases self-worth on material things. Looking to external rewards for our self-worth keeps us dependent on society's approval. We keep buying more, getting more education, accomplishing more, and working harder, but we cannot feel a sense of satisfaction. Self-worth originates within us. In spiritual terms, it is recognition of the sacred presence with us. We are dependent on others in our early life to help us in developing our self-esteem. We take our cues from our caretakers. If they are unable to reflect our worth to us or are overtly abusive, we struggle with self-esteem throughout life until we take steps to heal it. While there is no substitute for self-worth, it is a great gift when others treat us respectfully. Such moments are full of grace and can awaken our instinctive sense of self-respect and start us on a healing path.

Where are you on the following scale? In which direction are you moving?

Externally Focused <————————> Internally Focused

The emerging matrix of wholeness brings a message of hope; it has the possibility of binding us together and binding our cultural wounds. It breaks through the imagined dichotomies that have separated us for so long. It has the blueprints for the earth community that we know in our hearts is right. After you have read Chapter 25—"Setting Your Internal Compass"—and have identified what is most important to you, come back to this chapter and notice how well our culture represents or fails to represent your values. Living your values even when society does not reflect them is demanding, and it is intrinsic to living authentically.

INSIDE THE MEDICINE BAG:
Tools for Awakening Consciousness

Asking yourself thought-provoking questions brings your subconscious closer to the surface, thereby helping you to discover your personal truth. So, ask yourself the following questions, being sure to dig really deep to locate the most honest answers you can find. If you have a journal, feel free to journal your responses. If you are part of a group, consider sharing.

- What is your personal experience of the cultural matrix? How does it feel?
- What parts of the existing cultural matrix do you disagree with?
- What parts of the existing cultural matrix do you agree with?
- How is the emerging matrix influencing your life? How does it feel?
- If you could design a cultural matrix, how would it be structured?
- How would it feel if you believed we are collectively dreaming a "new and improved" matrix?
- Describe your connection to your intuition and instinct.
- Think of a situation in which your intuition bumped into your sense of logic. How did you resolve this conflict? How did that feel?

CHAPTER 20

Assessing Your
Truth and Living It

*"Hell, in my opinion, is never finding your true self and
never living your own life or knowing who you are."*

—John Bradshaw (1933–), American author, counselor, and theologian

F*amily of origin* is a term frequently used in recovery circles,
especially with regard to dysfunctional families and how
they affect our development and self-worth. While we all
have a family of origin, we don't all have to think of them as totally
dysfunctional—perhaps capable of freaky moments is a better description of yours. Regardless of how you describe your family, it's good
to know that you can change your *experience* of it. You can heal the
leftover negative memories and your reactions to them. Identifying
the dynamics is the first step in making this transformational journey.

In the late 1980s, counselor and author John Bradshaw began decoding the family-of-origin mystery in his seminal work *On the Family: A Revolutionary Way of Self-Discovery*. This was followed by a host of books defining the "dysfunctional family system"—a group Bradshaw estimated to be 96 percent of the population. That wasn't all that long ago, and Bradshaw's theories and figures haven't been successfully challenged.

Some of the results of growing up in a dysfunctional family include poor self-image, fear, risky behavior, addiction, compulsion, difficulty focusing, hypervigilance, caretaking at the expense of self, perfectionism, being hard-hearted or caring too much, depression, and anxiety. It's fair to say if you grew up in a dysfunctional family, you are not alone!

The family matrix many of us have grown up with resembles the cultural matrix for the most part. Rather than laws, it is passed along in family stories, many of which have been handed down through the generations. These stories shape our thoughts, beliefs, and expectations according to a system of undeclared assumptions. They go a long way toward creating our identity, shaping our dreams, and defining our behavior. Like the cultural matrix, not much is based on how we feel—what is on our internal map, our heart. Rather, it hands us preconceived definitions and declarations. *"We do this. . . . We don't do that. . . . Men don't. . . . Women do. . . . Grown-ups do. . . . Children don't. . . ."* You know how this works.

Family is important, and legacies can empower you or drive you crazy and everything in between. We need to sort through the messages to find our truth. Maybe you aren't "just like your mother" or "just like your father" or "just like your uncle from Nebraska who drinks too much." Unless these stories resonate with your core being, they are up for a rethink. Examining these assumptions and discarding those that don't hold up to your scrutiny is a bold step that is ultimately and intricately bound to reclaiming your authenticity.

A good way of making this assessment is to pay attention to how certain family sayings affect your emotions. Do certain stories make you feel embarrassed? Do some make you feel proud? Are you encouraged in your pursuits or do you feel put down? You have a right to feel good about yourself. Validating your experience gives you permission to get more honest. You will be surprised at what you discover about yourself. You don't have to confront your family in the process; you are going for self-honesty.

> *My family wasn't into money and glamour; they were cracker pioneer, sweat blood, and get-the-job kind of people. Life was hard, and they were harder. I must have heard ten thousand times growing up, "Git up, get with it, or get out of my way!" I tried to be their way, but I couldn't make it work. So I believed I was less than. After all, a man was a man, and I felt like a mouse. I learned early how to be sneaky and sly. I never figured out who I was, me, Lee.*
>
> —From Lee's Story

Transforming the Past: Self-Image Redo

While we can't change the past, we can change *how we feel about ourselves* based on the past. That's an important distinction, and it bears repeating. You can change how you feel about yourself. Regardless of the kind of craziness that went on in your home, you absorbed it and have held yourself responsible for causing it. Kids are like that—they take on whatever is happening around them, and they think it's about them. Feelings of responsibility, anger, guilt, and shame are among the common results of growing up in family dysfunction. It may take professional help to heal, but you *can* heal—and, as you heal, you discover that you are much more than your old beliefs indicate.

As you begin this journey of self-discovery, it's helpful to learn the difference between guilt and shame, as the two are often confused. A common description says that guilt is feeling bad about something you *did*. It is a human emotion that can be helpful in building empathy. We feel bad about something we've done and we correct our behavior and we no longer feel guilty—as long as we include self-forgiveness. Shame is feeling that you *are* bad—so bad you can't be helped and forgiveness is totally off the table. It is difficult to resolve shame on your own, but it can be resolved with professional help, such as talking with a counselor or a spiritual advisor. While tackling family of origin dynamics can seem, at times, like climbing Mt. Everest barefooted, as you refuse to be defined by others and by the past, you get a boost in energy and transformation takes a quantum leap forward.

Coming to terms with addictions, obsessions, and compulsions that disconnect us from our truth and sabotage happiness is the beginning of building a solid core from the inside out—it's the beginning of authenticity. Being willing to believe in yourself, believe in your basic goodness, and believe in your right to your hopes and dreams are grist in the transformational mill.

Every human capacity exists on our hard drive—our internal computer. It's all there waiting to be downloaded. For example, we have the capacity to speak every language if we hear it early enough. It's all about what gets reinforced and what doesn't. Few of us were taught how to make decisions, including deciding who we are. We didn't get instructions on how to weigh options and select what is most appropriate for us in various situations. We were taught along strict lines of right and wrong—according to someone else's assessment, and acting right carried heavy moral consequences. Failure to follow the rules often led to guilt and shame and punishment from mild to severe. It may keep us in line, at least for a time, but it does not develop our soul or the empathy needed to be in intimate relationships with ourselves and others.

Empathy is on our internal compass—not in the codependent sense, but in true caring and connection with our self and with the human family. Empathy creates a moral map that we will rely on for making decisions throughout life. Empathy is developed naturally through the sensitive and loving care we receive in childhood. If we were not treated sensitively as a child, we can develop empathy later in life by changing our relationship to ourselves and learning to treat ourselves respectfully. That includes cleaning up destructive self-talk, refusing to buy into the negative stories we have heard about ourselves, and beginning to write our new story. While this sounds simple, it is not easy to override the early programming we receive—but it is entirely possible!

None of this is about blaming your family or yourself; it's about cutting through the inaccuracies—or, more to the point, lies—and finding out who you are when you have the pen in your hand, when you're telling the story. We often discover that we aren't much different from everyone else—but it's an *important* difference. We became what we were taught to believe we were—now we can become what *we* believe we are. Welcome to your new matrix.

Making an Essential Connection to Truth

Our genetic makeup changes as we assess the truth about ourselves and about life and begin living it. According to David R. Hamilton specialist in biological chemistry, we are more powerful than we think. Or you might say we are as *powerful as we think*. Hamilton considers the mind as a *force*, in that the mind's focus can bring about biological and physiological effects in the brain and body. He goes on to say,

"Thinking leads to activation and deactivation in the genes" in what he calls mind-gene interface. Connecting with the truth of our power is our spiritual right and our responsibility.

> *You can take responsibility for yourself and create your life with aware-*
> *ness, or you can continue to dance to whatever's on the jukebox.*

—From Lee's Story

Transformation calls us deeper within to make that essential connection to our core. This newfound source of power invites us to reevaluate assumptions and beliefs about self and about life with renewed confidence. In recovery, we draw a line in the sand between then and now. We choose honesty, and honesty begins within—when we tell ourselves the truth and make every effort to by live it. There is power in taking responsibility for our beliefs and for living true to them—and yes, it can be challenging! But authenticity is worth it. While no one follows his or her code perfectly, dedication to living as clean as possible constitutes living authentically.

In 12-Step recovery, there is an ongoing assessment in which the day is reviewed and mistakes are quickly corrected by admitting to the mistake and taking responsibility for it. (*Step 10. Continued to take personal inventory and when we were wrong, promptly admitted it.*) Through self-reflective practices such as this, authenticity becomes a way of living, not a one-time accomplishment. In taking a daily inventory, we suggest marking the things you did right and appreciating them as well as identifying areas where you want to improve. If you are recovering from a negative self-image, focus on what you did right for at least a month (and maybe longer) to help create balance. You'll recognize the balance point when your resistance to saying nice things about yourself goes away, and you begin enjoying it—without feeling guilty.

Big Wheel Keep on Turning

Your family matrix probably reflects the cultural matrix in many ways. It's a chicken-and-egg situation. Families reflect culture, and culture reflects families. Breaking out of the existing matrix can take more energy than staying in it, yet truth demands expression. New ideas are always breaking into the mainstream, and the dictionary adds new words every year; people dance to new music each generation and societal rules change, and, yes, your family can, too—or at least one member can . . . you! An inflexible matrix based on absolutism cannot stand up to the greater forces of nature, such as creativity and human expression. You've got the big forces of nature on your side.

Holding fast against the tides of change offers security, but it is a false sense of safety. It is not based in truth. In truth, we keep re-creating ourselves. We change, traditions change, rules change, and the laws change. At the same time, stability matters. In holism, each thing contains its opposite. The principle of change exists only in relationship to the principle of unchanging and vice versa. One is not right and the other wrong; resisting change is as natural as pushing for it.

The first obstacle to happiness was my belief in needing to fit in. The belief that fitting in would bring happiness made me inauthentic. From that point forward, I sought validation from the world that I was good enough. I became a chameleon—changing my look, my talk, and my angle depending on whomever I was with or where I was. Just being me was not good enough. I had to be bigger and better.

—From Lee's Story

Change is stressful. It's a lot less stressful when you understand the dynamics involved. We each carry the seeds of transformation. Our intention is to assist you in getting yours planted. Chances are you are dreaming a different dream from your family and mainstream society.

When you know what you're up against, you can bring your dream into reality much easier than when you're operating in the dark. History is on the side of change, but not change for the sake of it—you know, stirring things up just to get a reaction. We need conscious change, honest change—the kind that originates deep inside. As is often the case, *one* person in the family gets honest, and, through his or her authenticity, the family dynamics begin to change. If you are the one who "gets it," the path can be lonely, but it's worth it. It's harder to go against your newfound awareness than to move ahead with it. Trust yourself and your connection to Spirit. You'll find your people.

INSIDE THE MEDICINE BAG:
Tools for Awakening Consciousness

Asking yourself thought-provoking questions brings your subconscious closer to the surface, thereby helping you to discover your personal truth. So, ask yourself the following questions, being sure to dig really deep to locate the most honest answers you can find. If you have a journal, feel free to journal your responses. If you are part of a group, consider sharing.

- What are some beliefs in your family that come from the cultural matrix?
- What was the family "story" about you? How does it make you feel?
- If you would like a new story, what would it be? How does it feel?
- How would you feel about writing your own story?
- Write your new story the way you want it to be.
- What does it feel like as you share it?
- Stand up and walk around the room as the new you. How does the new you feel?

Exercise—Dream Board

Make a dream board that illustrates your new story—not based on the past or upon your family's beliefs and expectations, but on your own truth. Gather images from magazines, posters, or old greeting cards that represent what you would like to bring into your life. The images can reflect feelings you would like to have as well as "things." Glue them onto poster paper and share it with your group or with a friend. Place it where you'll see it regularly. Your subconscious mind works with images—pictures of what you want it to create. Each time the image bounces off your retina, you are closer to having your new dream become your reality.

CHAPTER 21

Traveling the Circles of Life

*"Everything that slows us down and
forces patience, everything that sets us back
in to the slow circles of nature is a help."*

—May Sarton (1912–1995), American poet and novelist

There are no straight lines in nature—no beginnings without endings and no endings without beginnings. However, much of Western culture and particularly American culture is based on a linear construct, in which time and life are experienced on a trajectory from a beginning point to an end point. This model doesn't reflect the cyclical nature of life nor its connectedness.

Nature is cyclical. In comparison to linear time, a circular model reflects an interrelated and interconnected whole. It reflects reality.

Our round earth spins in circles as it orbits around the sun. The burning disk in the sky creates days and nights and seasons come, go, and return again. The moon appears as a tiny sliver, growing round before our eyes, and slowly disappearing back into the darkness, only to reappear a few nights later to repeat its pattern.

Cyclical time reflects our internal cycle, which balances the flow of our life energy taking us through periods of activity and times of rest. *Doing* uses energy. When we *overdo,* our life force runs low, leaving little or none for healing. Healing is about *being*—what we know as downtime. *Being* recharges our battery. It is important to cultivate practices that help us maintain a balance between doing and being. In this chapter, we'll look at some time-honored ways that promote inner balance and support peace of mind even as we meet today's demands.

Mandala Wisdom

Meditation is the best and most economical way of balancing the brain and creating good health at all levels—body, mind, and spirit. It's particularly helpful when making the kind of changes we're describing in this book. Sitting still and observing the mind, while it doesn't cost any money, is challenging especially as a newcomer to the practice. A mandala is a very old and helpful tool to begin this exploring meditation.

The word *mandala* comes from the ancient Sanskrit language of India and means *circle.* In its simplest form, a mandala is a geometric form containing pictures, colors, or designs. At other levels, it is an experience; it symbolizes the universe—both the external universe in which we live and the internal one inside us, creating harmony between them.

Mandala Pattern

Centering in the Mandala

The integrated pattern inside a mandala is organized around a unifying center—organic to how we orientate ourselves. We speak of family circles, our circle of friends, and social circles, and refer to being inside the circle or outside the circle. We feel peaceful and centered as we contemplate a mandala—our mind and body rest in the circle. It is like coming home to one's self.

In the Americas, native people create medicine wheels and sand mandalas. The circular Aztec calendar is both a timekeeping device and a religious expression. The yin-yang symbol of Asian culture honors creation as both male and female and places the symbol inside a circular construct. Tibetan mandalas are the focus of meditation. Their detailed designs symbolize wholeness and belonging. The circle is rooted in our unconscious mind; it is sacred geometry.

The labyrinth is a popular mandala pattern dating back to Neolithic time, and perhaps earlier. Today it can be found in the local church-yard where a modern day spiritual seeker can walk its ancient twists and turns. Labyrinths are sometimes confused with mazes, but they are fundamentally different patterns with different effects. A maze is designed to confuse the person who enters it. A labyrinth guides you through a series of switchbacks, taking you to the center where you experience being in your own center. If you enter the labyrinth with a question, its illogical pattern allows you to let go of your thinking mind and relax into the rhythm of the circle. As you stand in the center, you find your personal center—where you often discover a new piece of your truth. The way out of the labyrinth takes you back through the twists and turns, providing integration and often bringing further insight. Others simply enjoy walking the pathways and relaxing.

Chartres Cathedral Labyrinth

You can possibly find a labyrinth in your town by searching online, or you can get together with friends and explore creating one of your own. The winding circular pattern of the labyrinth helps balance the hemispheres of brain, quieting the mind and calming the body. Once the static is off your internal wires, insight continues long after you finish your walk.

That is life, isn't it? To either choose from the heart what we aspire to or settle for the world's version of what we would be if we are willing to believe that something outside ourselves would know better than we do. After having believed that life was a great maze, I now found myself in more of a labyrinth. A labyrinth leads back to the center rather than to the outside, as a maze does. It was my center that I had been missing.

—From Lee's Story

Earth's Calendar

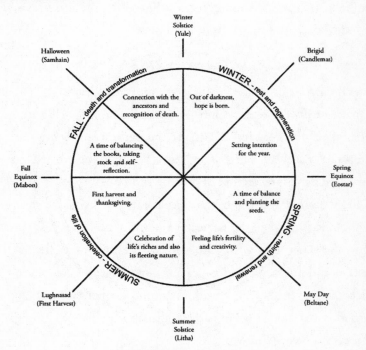

Wheel of the Year

This calendar dates back to at least 2000 BCE, and corresponds to the seasons of the year in Europe where it originated. It relates to similar latitudes throughout much of North America. It is generally attributed to the Celtic people from a time in history when it was understood that nature contained the sacred. Today, people all over the world continue the tradition of gathering to observe the unique relationship between the sun and the earth that occurs on solstices and equinoxes. The modern-day liturgical calendar of religious feasts is based on this ancient calendar.

Following is a brief walk through the earth calendar year along with spiritual teachings of each season. The information has been intuited over thousands of years and is common to many people and cultures. At the same time, it is open for new insight. Notice your reactions and any "aha's" you might have as you read.

Winter Solstice or Yule (December 21–23)

Winter solstice marks the darkest time of the year in the northern hemisphere. It draws us within—a time of dreaming. This is nature's shortest day and longest night. At the darkest moment, when the sun is farthest away, it begins its journey back to the Northern sky. It symbolizes the intersection of despair and hope.

In modern times, we continue to celebrate Hanukkah, the festival of lights, Christmas, and the African-American tradition of Kwanzaa— all lifting our spirits with gathering with family and friends, food, candles and lights. Consider clearing time after the preparation and celebration of the holidays for doing nothing—perhaps relaxing with a good book—or gathering for a potluck supper with friends and watching a favorite movie.

Candlemas or Bridget's Day (February 2)

Candlemas marks the midway point between winter solstice and spring equinox. The light is returning; the end of winter is in sight. As you begin to notice the days getting longer, you feel your spirit lifting. Your mind shifts from thinking that winter will never end to looking forward to what's coming next.

In Gaelic, this feast is called *Oimelc*, meaning "ewe's milk," signifying that the new lambs have arrived—and life is returning. It was a time when the Goddess Brighid (Gaelic for Bridget) was celebrated. When Ireland converted to Christianity, it proved difficult to get rid of all the old gods and goddesses, and Brighid was a favorite. The church transformed her into Saint Bridget, and she is celebrated around the world. Spiritually, this preview of spring rewards hope acknowledging new life. Spring planting will soon begin.

Candlemas reminds us about holding still and waiting for the inevitable shift in consciousness—rather than thinking you have to know something before you know it. Consider describing in your journal what it is like for you to wait for an answer to emerge from your deep knowing. And describe how it feels when it finally does emerge.

Spring Equinox (March 20–23)

The spring equinox, also known as Easter, is a time of physical and spiritual rebirth. Daylight is lengthening. Nature has made good on her promise; what died in winter now resurrects. As new green sprouts push up through the warming earth, consciousness awakens to new possibilities. Spring transmits a spirituality of new beginnings—it reminds us that no matter how dark the journey the light returns. We heal and life continues.

It's time to consider what you want to plant in the field or the garden and in your internal life as well. What values do you want to nurture? At the equinox, day and night are of equal length—symbolizing balance. You might use it to take an inventory of how you spend your energy, noticing whether you give too much of yourself away or hold back.

May Day or Beltane (April 30–May 1)

Beltane celebrates fertility. In the old days Maypoles were built as phallic symbols, and young couples danced around them, weaving ribbons together in mating rituals. It was believed that the energy generated was danced down into the earth to enhance the fruitfulness of the fields. This practice continues today. Spiritually, it honors the balance of male and female and the sacredness of sexuality and new life.

May Day celebrates nature's power of renewal. You might notice what is awakening in you as spring moves into its fullness. What hope or dream is asking to be born? This is a good time to energize it. The same energy that is bursting everywhere around you can help manifest a dream.

Summer Solstice or Litha (June 21–23)

Summer is a metaphor for happy, joyous, and free. Long sunlit summer days and warm temperatures call for playtime. Seeds that were planted in spring are now healthy strong plants watered by summer rain and thriving. Tomatoes ripen and flowers bloom. Life is good. Summer fills our inner storehouse with pleasant days and nights to be remembered during the tough times. Spiritually, it brings the fulfillment of hope—the presence of the Sacred in nature can be trusted. We are cared for.

Everything in nature is telling us to "cool it." Make sure your fun quotient is filled. Perhaps explore a new summer activity or rediscover one you have almost forgotten. Run through the sprinkler, sleep outside, or invite friends over to eat watermelon.

Lughnasadh or First Harvest (August 1)

Lughnasadh celebrates first harvest. Communities gather to enjoy thanksgiving festivals otherwise known as end of summer picnics. The light that was growing at Candlemas is now waning. Lughnasadh celebrates abundance, evoking the spirit of gratitude. And it reminds us of the temporal nature of life, as the days grow shorter.

First harvest invites us to enjoy the bounty of the garden—to reap what we have sown. Metaphorically it reminds us to honor our accomplishments. Shop at your local farmers market. Have a picnic. Make a gratitude list.

Fall Equinox or Mabon (September 21–23)

Fall equinox is another opportunity for rebalancing. Like spring equinox, the days and nights are of the same length, but now the balance is leaning toward darkness. Fall shifts our attention from the fullness of life to the realization of endings. Spiritually, it reinforces the ultimate wisdom of letting go. Days shorten, and evenings grow cool. It's a time to light the fire again and put on the soup. Wild geese fly overhead, and we long to fly with them—to escape the inevitable approaching cold. Spiritually, this is a time of reflection on cycles of life as the green of the fields turns to gold and days shorten.

It's a time of taking stock of what is important to us and perhaps refining our priorities.

Samhain or Halloween (October 31)

Samhain or Halloween, as it is known today, offers a radical confrontation with death. But it puts a friendly face on what we most fear by celebrating the return of the ancestors. It is believed that the veil between the worlds is temporally lifted and the souls of the dead revisit the earth at this time.

Spiritually, it provides an opportunity to reflect on the great mystery of death and to recognize that life continues in its transformed way—at least that is our hope. Halloween symbolizes the end of the year taking us through fall and easing us into winter. What are you willing to put on your altar to be transformed?

Balance and Order

Familiarity with the wheel of life allows us to penetrate life's greatest mysteries—birth and death and rebirth . . . and all that goes in between. It is a study in balance. As you look at the feasts on the wheel, notice the interplay of opposites. Winter, when the earth has shut down, sits across from summer's fullness of life. Candlemas, the time of early planting, sits across from fall and the first harvest. Spring equinox, as the light returns to the sky, sits across from fall equinox, as we head back into darkness. Beltane, with all its lusty fertility, sits across from death. Organically grounded, there is no separation between spirit and body on the wheel of life.

Working with the innate spirituality of the forces of nature and the lessons they carry can make the journey more meaningful. It lets you know that God is present in the light and in the shadows all the time. It makes qualities like faith, hope, joy, trust, and nurturing—even fear and loss—tangible, and experience rather than simply just words or ideas.

Awakening Innate Intelligence—the Miracle of Us

Migration and hibernation patterns, seeds sprouting from the soil and ending up on your dinner table, and even the leaves on trees turning color as the days shorten—all teach us about our organic connection to nature and awakens life-affirming consciousness.

Animals demonstrate this powerful connection. For example, grizzly bears hibernate within a few hours of each other on the day the real winter freeze occurs, ignoring cold snaps while waiting for the hard freeze. Migrating birds are attuned to energy lines in the earth, which guide them along their amazing journeys. And, each year, salmon swim thousands of miles to return to their birthplace and spawn the next generation. Perhaps one of the most amazing migrations is that of the monarch butterflies who travel up to 2,500 miles to the same trees every year. Even more astonishing is that they aren't the same butterflies from year to year.

While this is all very interesting, you may be wondering, *What has it got to do with me and my transformation?* It's about recognizing and realizing the incredible smarts that have been packed into those fragile little butterfly wings—and all the animals—exist in you, too. Their patterns are our patterns.

The Earth pulses with the divine intelligence of the creator. She takes care of her children—and we are hers. As you awaken to the absolute miracle of your physical body, abusing it loses its charm. We are recovering from the broken connection between body and soul and the teachings that disrespected the beauty and intelligence of the body telling us the Sacred lived somewhere other than here with us. As our awareness of the Spirit's presence within us grows, our self-appreciation and deep respect for life increases.

INSIDE THE MEDICINE BAG:
Tools for Awakening Consciousness

Engaging in meditative practices brings your subconscious closer to the surface, thereby helping you to discover your personal truth. Consider the following activities as a path inward for awakening your authentic self.

- Create your own mandala using colored pencils, crayons, or paint. You can find patterns online, to print and color. Spending time with this ancient pattern is healing. Notice how soothing it is to sit quietly and color a mandala. This activity calms your nervous system and fosters a feeling that everything is okay. It opens the mind to receive insight and it strengthens intuition and your immune system.

- Make your own earth calendar and mark the festivals as described in this chapter. Meditate on the seasons and identify the spiritual principles shown on our earth calendar as they resonate with you. Discover new insights and add them to your calendar.

Exercise—The Incan Sun Salute

- Of all the circles of life, the sun is the most significant. The sun energizes all life on earth. Spiritual guide and Incan teacher Jorge Luis Delgado shares a bit of Inca cosmology in his book *Andean Awakening: An Inca Guide to Mystical Peru*. In the spiritual tradition of the Inca, we are all Children of the Sun. The Inca believe the sun we see is fed by the Sun Behind the Sun or Divine Presence, sending light and love through Father Sun to Mother Earth to nourish the children

and all creation. In his book, Delgado suggests the following
life-changing meditation for those who would like to experience
this ancient Incan practice. Jorge recommends doing this every
day for several months and noticing how your life changes.
Then consider making it a lifelong practice. As always this is
an invitation.

*Each day as you wake up go outside and greet the sun. Be in gratitude
of living another day here in creation. Facing Father Sun, open your arms
wide and feel the warmth on your face, on your chest and in your heart.
All life on earth is sustained by the energy of the sun. Be aware of the gift
of life and be grateful. Place one hand over your heart, breathe deeply and
say "all my love." Take a moment to feel the words. Place the other hand
on your stomach, breathe deeply, and say "without fear." Do this slowly
and with intention, feeling the meaning behind the words you are saying and feeling what you are doing. If you notice any heaviness around
your midsection, brush it off, sending it down to the Mother Earth. The
Mother Earth transforms our fears and anxieties like a mother wipes
away tears and calms her children.*

- Notice the location of the sun throughout the day—in what
  part of your yard it shines at various times. Notice the shadows
  as well. Notice how various times of day and evening effect
  your mood and your energy. What is happening "outside" us
  resonates inside us—and awakens awareness. In our awakened
  state, we become more conscious of the choices we make. This
  is the transformational journey.

Group Activities

- Allow time for each person in the group to create a mandala that represents the important aspects of his or her life journey. Use magic markers, paint, or clippings from magazines, and arrange the collage in a circular pattern. As a group, create a larger mandala by placing all of the individual mandalas in a circular pattern in the middle of the group circle. Invite each person in the group to tell the others what his or her picture represents. Allow a time of silence in which the group contemplates the group mandala. Invite each person to share his or her insight—keeping it brief and avoiding going into the old story.

- Organize the chairs in the room in a circle. Share your responses to the mandala exercise or introduce some other topic for group discussion. Observe how it feels to sit in a circle while sharing. Notice the flow of energy, ideas, and interactions. About midway through the discussion, organize the room in rows all facing in the same direction and continue sharing. Notice how this construct feels. Notice the flow of energy, ideas, and interactions.

Discuss the differences between sitting in a circle and sitting in rows. Value each person's experience as they share it with the group by listening carefully and contemplating its meaning to you.

CHAPTER 22

Meditating with Nature

*"God is found in silence. See how nature—trees,
flowers, grass—grows in silence; see how the stars,
the moon and the sun, how they move in silence.
We need silence to be able to touch souls."*

—Mother Teresa (1910–1997), Catholic nun,
humanitarian, Nobel Peace Prize winner

We've been talking about how essential it is to have a conscious connection with nature to bring about our personal healing and transformation. The Gaia Hypothesis drives home this truth even more so. This theory, which was named for the ancient primordial earth goddess—Gaia—was developed by scientist and inventor Dr. James Lovelock in the late 1960s. Lovelock's theory recognizes the earth as an integrated living and breathing organism that possesses intelligence and consciousness.

Earth regulates global temperature, atmospheric content, ocean salinity, and other factors that sustain both our planet and us as one unified living system. Over the years scientists have identified many of these self-regulating systems, supporting Lovelock's theory and affirming the intuitive wisdom of many of the ancient stories.

Today, we may refer to Gaia (she from whom all creation ascended) as Mother Nature or Earth Mother—the symbol of the living presence in nature. Addiction is about disconnection—disconnection from our bodies, from our emotions, from the people we loved and from life itself. Recovery is about connection and presence, getting back in touch, back in our bodies, back down to earth. In her form as Sacred Tree, Gaia stands as a beacon, calling us home and grounding us in her roots.

Rooting with Nature

To access the healing power of Gaia and ground yourself to the earth, start by finding a tree that "calls your name." A tree calls your name by making itself noticeable, looking especially beautiful, offering shade from the heat, or somehow getting your attention. You will be building a relationship with this tree. Find one that offers you strength or tenderness or beauty or power or for any other reason, whether you can explain it or not. It can be in your yard or park or anywhere that you can sit by it without being interrupted. If you are housebound or for some other reason find it difficult to find a tree, a plant will do. In a pinch, a picture of one will work. The tree as a spiritual archetype appears in all cultures. Shamans use the image of a tree to travel to the upper and underworlds. The Tree of Knowledge is a primary symbol in Judeo/Christian tradition. Trees are one of the first figures children draw.

Trees are respected in the world of herbal and flower medicine for their wisdom and healing abilities. Old trees have grandparent energy. Rings of the tree contain a record of the weather patterns as well as events that occurred near them for as long as they have been alive. In this regard, you can say the tree is sensate—it has emotions and memory—not in a human way but in a tree way.

Sit with your tree friend for a half hour at least twice a week. Lean against the trunk and feel the support. Lean into it like you would lean into a loving grandparent. Allow Grandparent Tree to relax your back, your shoulders, and your brain. Feel peace as it flows from the tree to you. Tell the tree your story. You can do that as you sit by it and write in your journal. You can even read it to the tree out loud.

Notice the life that goes on in and around the tree—birds, insects, squirrels, and the circle of shade beneath it and what grows near it. Become familiar with the life systems that rely on the tree and consider yourself a part of this community—you are dependent on it for the very air you breathe. Find out what kind of a tree it is and learn about it. As your relationship with the tree grows, you can take problems to it and find comfort there. Trees are wisdom carriers. You will find solutions to your problems by meditating with the tree (see the grounding meditation below). As the image of the tree takes root in your subconscious mind, you can connect with the tree anytime from anyplace and have your support system at hand.

> *If I told you that the land showed me what I was to do with it, I would not be telling tales. It didn't tell me in words; it told me in love and in the experience of working those equine programs. I knew I was supposed to do something. I knew those ranches were about more than just running cows. Then I got it. The ranches I lived on offered a perfect setting for a residential healing/treatment program.*
>
> —From Lee's Story

Grounding Tree Meditation

Establish mutual respect in your relationship by asking the tree if it will participate in your meditation. Notice the spread of its branches, and be aware that its root system occupies the same space underground as its branches aboveground. Lean against the tree trunk, close your eyes, and imagine being the tree.

Feel what it would be like to be deeply rooted in the ground like the tree. Let your energy follow the trunk of the tree into the ground and expand into the root system. Feel it. Next, follow the tree trunk up into the branches and notice what it's like to be sky bound. What does it feel like to provide safety and comfort to the world of creatures?

Next, change places in your mind and become one of the creatures that finds shelter in the tree—a rabbit perhaps. Feel what it's like to burrow in among the tree roots and curl up for the night wrapped in Mother Earth. Imagine a whole system of tunnels where you and the other creatures live. Notice how it feels to live down underground. Now, become a bird and take your attention upward into the branches. Notice how it feels to nest in the arms of the Mother Tree.

Bring your attention back to your body, but leave your roots in the ground. Breathe into your roots and then begin to pull the earth energy up into your body. Imagine this source of healing energy as a color and a temperature. What type of healing energy does it provide for you? Restful? Peaceful? Trustful? Slowly fill up your body with this root energy and feel what it brings you. Next, bring your attention into the branches. Pull the sky energy into your body. Notice the color, texture, and temperature. Slowly fill up your body with this sky energy and feel what it brings you. After sitting by your tree and talking with it several times, it will ground you from anywhere anytime by simply imagining it. Now, thank the tree.

None of this makes sense to your thinking mind—and that's the point. It relaxes your brain and puts you in your imagination where you can heal. You can't think yourself well; you can only relax and allow your healing to happen.

Ten Reasons to Be Grateful for Trees

The more time we spend with and around trees, the more our appreciation for them grows (as well as our appreciation for ourselves). But since we live in a culture that often requires "proof," we're offering you the many reasons to be grateful for these generous and beautiful beings. The following top ten reasons trees are valuable from a scientific point of view was compiled by professional forester and natural resource consultant Steve Nix.*

Nix's top ten reasons are 1) Trees produce oxygen. 2) Trees clean the soil. 3) Trees control noise pollution. 4) Trees slow storm water runoff. 5) Trees are carbon sinks. 6) Trees clean the air. 7) Trees shade and cool. 8) Trees act as windbreaks. 9) Trees fight soil erosion. 10) Trees increase property value.

We literally depend on trees for our lives. Forests acts as giant filters that clean the air we breathe. And like us, trees breathe—they "inhale" or take in sunlight, water, and carbon dioxide to nourish them and, in turn, "exhale" oxygen into the atmosphere. A mature leafy tree produces as much oxygen in one season as ten people inhale in a whole year.

Trees store harmful pollutants and render them less harmful. For example, trees filter sewage and farm chemicals, reduce the effects of animal wastes, clean roadside spills, and purify water runoff before it enters the streams. Trees reduce pollution by filtering the air, reducing heat, and absorbing pollutants like carbon monoxide, sulfur dioxide, and nitrogen dioxide. They

* From: http://forestry.about.com/od/treephysiology/tp/tree_value.htm.

even muffle urban noise almost as effectively as stonewalls. Planted in the neighborhood or around the house, trees can significantly reduce noises from freeways and airports, as well.

Trees can also dramatically reduce the harmful effects of flash flooding. For example, a single fully grown Colorado blue spruce can intercept more than 1,000 gallons of water annually. Trees also slow runoff and refill underground aquifers. As far as global warming is concerned, trees absorb and lock carbon dioxide (a global-warming suspect) in their wood, roots, and leaves. This means less carbon dioxide is available for contribution to the greenhouse effect.

Also, shade trees reduce the need for air conditioning in hot weather, as they can reduce the inside temperature by as much as 12 degrees. And in cold weather, trees act as windbreaks, potentially lowering home heating bills by up to 30 percent. Moreover, reducing wind reduces the drying effect on soil and vegetation and helps keep topsoil from blowing away. Trees fight erosion by binding the soil with their roots. They conserve rainwater and reduce water runoff and sediment deposit after storms. And as we all know, trees beautify a property or neighborhood and can actually increase the property value of a home by 15 percent or more.

That's plenty of reason to be grateful for these magnificent woody creatures.

Earth-Walking Meditation

Thich Nhat Hanh, Zen Buddhist monk, teacher, and author of *Peace Is Every Step* among many other books, teaches his students and readers about the sacredness of the earth, encouraging us to practice walking with consciousness of this sacredness. He says, "The practice of mindful walking is a profound and pleasurable way to deepen our connection with our body and the earth. We breathe, take a mindful step, and come back to our true home."

When practiced this way, every step we take can bring about profound healing. A walking meditation creates presence in our body, strengthens our awareness of the gift of life, and increases our awareness of the earth as a living being. As Thich Nhat Hanh reminds us, "Only when we are connected with our body are we truly alive." He offers the following suggestions for your earth-walking meditation:

Walk as if you are in a beautiful cathedral or temple or mosque. Notice every step that you take. Be aware of your feet touching the earth. Feel the pull of gravity as it secures you closer to her and holds you. Contemplate the miracle of the twenty-six bones in each of your feet working together to move you along your way. Walk slowly and breathe into each step. Feel the connection between you, the earth, your feet, and your breath.

You can practice your walking meditation on your own or with others. If possible, walk on the earth rather than on pavement. Walk in silence and focus on each slow step, allowing each foot to linger on the earth, breathing as you go.

The earth's biosphere includes the atmosphere that surrounds it, much like the aura, or field of energy, that surrounds our bodies. As you extend the image of earth to include its atmosphere, you are inside the earth—the ecosphere. Imagine yourself inside the earth's energy field, enveloped by her, supported by her, and fed and nurtured by her. Body and mind coexist as a unified being. The relationship between your body and your mind reflects your relationship with life. When they are respectful of one another, you feel peaceful.

Try the following mantra along with your walking meditation to bring the mind and body together in a peaceful partnership. Place one hand on your heart as you walk, slowly saying, "Peace be with you," on the inhalation. Then, on the exhalation, change hands and say, "And also with you," as if you are having a conversation between your mind and body. Sometimes it feels like your head and heart are at odds with each other. This will bring them into peaceful relationship.

Fire-Gazing Meditation

People have sat around the fire stirring it with a stick, sharing stories, laughing, and crying together since we first stole it from the gods. Sparks rise, and you follow them with your eyes as they disappear into the night sky, and you feel you are touching the stars.

Fire has the ability to both calm and energize us. A fire is the perfect atmosphere for meditation. The smell of wood burning, the glowing embers, and the snap and crackle of the flames combine and awaken an ancient consciousness. We find ourselves sitting on a saber-tooth tiger skin in front of the cave once again!

> *By the time I arrived [at the sweat lodge] the fire had already been burning for a couple of hours. I could see, between the layers of wood and ash, the stones glowing with the heat and spirit of the fire. . . . I was excited, nervous, self-conscious, and willing. Somehow I was familiar with the space as if I'd been there before. I felt in tune with the frequency of the place; my spirit knew where we were. I had no idea what I was doing; I just knew in my heart that this opportunity was a gift.*

> —From Lee's Story

A sweat lodge is a purification ritual and prayer form found in several cultures around the world. In this country, it's considered a Lakota tradition. Fire is a source of transformation, and, in the sweat lodge, the glowing red rocks in the center of the circle become a focus point for meditation. You can capture some of the power and mystery of the ancient ceremony by building your own fire and creating your own ceremony of cleansing and healing.

Find a safe place to build a fire outdoors or make a fire pit in your yard if that is permissible. If you aren't an experienced fire builder, have someone teach you about fire safety. If you don't have a suitable place to build a fire, a candle will do.

Light the flame, sit back, gaze into the fire, and relax as the magic of the flame slows your brain and draws your attention inside you. It isn't necessary to do anything. Don't worry about time; just let yourself be. Simply spending time with the fire is its own form of healing.

When you need to get rid of something, give it to the fire to be transformed. Simply write it down on a plain piece of paper, hold it in your hand until you feel ready to let it go, and then give it to the fire. As the paper turns to ashes, your "problem" begins to transform. Fire taps into deep memory, and you are able to let go at the subconscious level. Be open to a new experience as your relationship to the situation changes as a result of your experience.

Wonder-of-Water Meditation

Water works wonders with a worried mind. Sit by a body of water, and breathe and relax. You can do this as you soak in your bathtub or as you stand in the shower being aware of the water as it flows over your body. If you are sitting by moving water, feel it moving through you, giving you life. As it flows through you, it washes away any sorrow or pain. If you need something, ask the water to bring it to you. If you are in a particularly good space emotionally, send your positive vibrations downstream for others to share.

If you are sitting by still water, feel the same stillness within you. Breathe into your belly and connect your body with the body of water beside you. What do you imagine lies beneath the surface? Take a small rock or stone and breathe into it, connecting your life force with the stone. Breathe your gratitude into the water for the gift of life it brings. Gently drop the stone into the water and follow it down to the bottom in your imagination, until you are resting on the seabed.

A walk along the ocean shore quickly rearranges your molecules transforming stress and worry into peace and serenity. The salt spray, the ions, and the rhythm of the waves relax your mind and renew your body. It's difficult to remember what you were worrying about after a beach walk. If there is anything left of the old concern, dig a hole by the water's edge and bury it. Or write it in the sand. Go back out after the tide has turned and notice how the beach has been washed clean and smooth.

Sunset Meditation

Stories connect us to nature in a childlike way—to the time when we knew that the earth was alive. Our healing lies in reconnecting to this magical sense of life. It slows down the brain and our natural healing ability takes over.

We *know* that the Earth revolves around the sun, but we still experience the sun's rising and setting as if it revolves around the earth. It is possible to change this perspective so that you are experiencing the movement of the earth. The process can be magical. This sunset meditation comes to us from cosmologist and mathematician Brian Swimme: Take a blanket out to a place where you can see the sunset. Lie on your back on the blanket with your head pointed west into the setting sun. Tip your head back so you can see the sun as it sets. As it slips below the horizon, imagine that you are lying on the back of a huge turtle. Feel the movement of the earth as it rolls away from the sun. Remain still and notice any shifts in your perspective.

Enjoying the Rain

The weather reports have led us to think of rain as bad. You'll often hear the meteorologist say, "There will be good weather this weekend," meaning sunny. Or, "Sorry, there is more bad weather for the weekend," meaning rain. If you have ever watched your garden burn up for lack of water, you get a different sense of "good" weather.

Here's a practice that will reconnect you to your childhood when splashing in puddles was just plain fun. Go out in the rain and feel the drops as they hit your face. After the first shock, it might feel good. Stomp in the puddles. Get your feet wet and act like you don't care! If walking (and stomping) in the rain is new to you, don't worry—it's only water.

When you return home, take a shower and feel how good the warm water feels. After drying off, get comfortable and feel how alive your body feels. Consider calling your local television station to let them know that rain isn't the enemy!

Singing the Praises of the Creator and Creation

Exploring images of the sacred grounded in nature nourishes spiritual imagination. It personalizes our concept of the sacred and helps us as we begin to identify the God of our understanding and the unique way our God speaks to us. Investigation is part of our journey toward spiritual authenticity.

Following are prayers and poems from a variety of spiritualities. As you read through them, notice their effect on your imagination. When you find one that captures the sense of the sacred in a new and pleasing way, consider making it part of your daily prayer practice. After doing this for a week or two, notice how your relationship with Spirit has changed.

Awakening

THE EARTH IS AWAKENING.
SHE HAS BEEN SLEEPING.
BUT NIGHT IS ALMOST DONE
AND SHE IS WAKING UP.
DAWN IS LIGHTENING THE EAST.
NEW LIFE IS LIGHTING THE EAST.
NIGHT IS ALMOST DONE
AND ATIRA IS WAKING UP.

—Pawnee ritual for awakening the goddess Atira

Salute to Gaia—Earth Mother

OF HER I SING, THE ALL MOTHER,
OLD AND ROCK HARD AND BEAUTIFUL.
OF HER I SING, THE NOURISHER,
SHE UPON WHOM EVERYTHING FEEDS.
OF GAIA I SING. WHOEVER YOU ARE,
WHEREVER YOU ARE, SHE FEEDS YOU
FROM HER SACRED TREASURY OF LIFE.
BOUNTIFUL HARVESTS BEAUTIFUL
CHILDREN, THE FULLNESS OF LIFE:
THESE ARE HER GIFTS. PRAISE HER.

—Homeric hymn to Gaia

Song to Mountain Goddess

THERE IS SOMEONE WHO LIVES
IN THE FOLD OF THE MOUNTAINS.
SHE WEARS A COAT OF LEAVES
TRIMMED WITH SOFT RABBIT HAIR.
HER EYES LAUGH. SO DOES
HER MOUTH WITH ITS PEARL SMILE.
OH, HOW THE GODDESS
CALLS ME TO HER SIDE!
AND PLAYING THERE WITH HER,
HOW I FORGET TO RETURN!

—*Chinese Song to the Mountain Goddess*

Dancing for Joy

LOOK WHAT THE GODDESS DOES WHEN SHE IS SAD:
SHE TAKES UP A TAMBOURINE, MADE OF TAUT SKIN
AND RIMMED WITH CASTANETS OF BRASS,
AND SHE BEGINS TO DANCE. THE SOUND OF FLUTES
BLARES OUT WILDLY, REACHING EVEN TO THE DEPTHS
OF THE UNDERWORLD, SO LOUD, SO CLAMOROUS IS IT.
LOOK WHAT THE GODDESS DOES WHEN SHE IS SAD:
SHE FINDS THE WILDNESS IN HERSELF, AND AS SHE DOES,
SHE FINDS THAT THERE IS JOY THERE TOO.

—*Euripides, Greek dramatist. Readings from* The Goddess Companion
by Patricia Monaghan, Llewellyn Publishing, 2000.

Prayer to White Buffalo Woman

O HOLY ONE!

SHE WHO GAVE THE LAKOTA THE PEACE PIPE

TO CONNECT THEM TO ALL LIFE

GIVE ME THE ABILITY

TO CONNECT TO THE WORLD AROUND ME,

TO KNOW THE SPIRIT OF ALL THINGS,

AND TO LIVE MY LIFE IN PEACE WITH THEM.

TO KNOW AND HONOR THE SACRED IN THE WORLD.

—EXCERPTS FROM ORIGINAL INVOCATION BY PEACE WHITE-

HORSE, MARCH 15, 2011

INSIDE THE MEDICINE BAG:
Tools for Awakening Consciousness

- Are there spiritualities that have always interested you? If so, explore them. You may find them within your present religion, as most religions have different interpretations and different expressions. Or you may branch out. Trust your sense of this process. You will probably circle back and land not too far from where you started, but with a new understanding of the sacred. Learning about other spiritual expressions can help you discover your personal spiritual truth. Respecting the paths of others translates to respecting your own path. It means you can make a choice about your beliefs, which means you are more likely to live authentically. Spiritual curiosity, like curiosity about anything, opens our mind and heart. Spiritual investigation isn't a conversion experience; it is about learning about the world. You can come away with your same views about what you believe and realize there are other viewpoints. This is spiritual maturity.

- Where on earth would you like to go if you had a magic carpet? Visit your local library or get online and begin exploring this place. Learn about the people—their food, their religion, their music and dance . . . and more. Learn how they interact with the natural world and notice the effect this has on your relationship with nature.

- Choose a prayer or poem or write one of your own about your connection to the earth and commit to saying it every morning and evening for 28 days—through all the phases of the moon. Notice how an awareness of your surroundings increases.

- Consider collecting prayers and poetry honoring nature that are meaningful to you. With these, create a meditation book. Include photographs or drawings that express the feelings of the words.
- Take a walk in the park and notice the trees that grow in your part of the country. Collect the leaves. Trace or draw them and the configuration of the branches until you can identify at least three kinds of trees.
- Animals carry healing medicine. You don't just imagine feeling better when the cat is sleeping on your lap, you do feel better. The same is true when Fido is curled up by your chair, and you feel safe and secure. Horses have a special healing ability that Lee describes in the first part of this book. If you have the opportunity to participate in equine assisted therapy, we recommend it. In the meantime, go back and reread his story, paying special attention to the parts about the horses.

CHAPTER 23

Connecting the Dream in Your Heart to Reality

"I thank you, God, for this most amazing
day: for the leaping greenly spirits of trees
and for the blue dream of sky; and for everything
which is natural which is infinite which is yes."

—E. E. Cummings (1894–1962), American poet

Conscious recovery is about connecting to the dream in your heart and allowing it to materialize and become reality—in other words, making a conscious connection. We're suggesting that you practice conscious dreaming using the *green dream.*

The *green dream* is a dream of an inspirited universe where divine presence is everywhere. In this dream, we belong to Spirit—body and soul. Indigenous people in this country and all around the world have been holding this dream until we would awaken to it. You may have known it as a kid. The wisdom of beginning with the green dream becomes clearer as you read this chapter—it's your map to freedom.

[As a kid] I learned to create my own secret places . . . where I could be alone with the magic of the woods. I favored the swamps and the cypress ponds. Spirits dwell in those places where the shadows are long, and something's always moving out of the corner of your eye. Among those palmettos and oaks, I'd spy deer and squirrels, and, once, I'd even seen a panther. I'd pretend to be invisible and that I could sneak up on the animals and get close enough to touch them.

I loved being in the presence of the animals. They were surrounded by peace, magic, and mystery. In the mystery, I was free from the need to be good enough or correct. The mystery touched something inside me that was deep and clear like a cold clean spring of awareness, pure life without all the baggage of the adult human world.

—From Lee's Story

We tend to think of nature as something we walk around on or spend time in on the weekend; the *green dream* reminds us that we *are* nature. Every element found in the human body comes from earth. The earth feeds us, houses us, and creates the air that we breathe. And the earth as well as all creation, including humans, is infused with divine presence. To be unconscious of this relationship is to be out of relationship with self and out of relationship with life—it's risky business. In the *green dream*, we remember that body and spirit are one with the creator. This is when we are able to connect the dream in our hearts to the reality in which we live, where they come together, and we realize that we are one with everything, and, as such, we have all we've ever needed or wanted.

Your life force—that which creates and sustains you—is the living presence of Great Spirit. Whether you call this "all there is," God, Higher Power, Goddess, Yahweh, Spirit, Allah, or anything else, you are *in* it and *of* it—it lives in you. We are all *one being* in the cosmic, universal, omnipresent sense. *God is everywhere.* We learned this as children, and it means exactly what it says, *God is everywhere!* More than connected with, we are one with the universe, one another, with the trees, the rocks, the atmosphere, rivers and oceans, raindrops, and everything from those pesky mosquitoes to the most fierce mountain lion—we're in this together.

While you inhabit your piece of cosmic real estate, life is much bigger, more creative, and more interesting than you might have imagined.

Commitment to a Transformed Relationship

In the old dream of Western culture, people assume rights over nature. This allows us to use resources for our benefit without understanding reciprocity and our complete dependence on keeping a balanced equation between ourselves and the rest of "it." Expecting the earth to meet all our needs without taking responsibility for our behavior is an addictive relationship.

> *Having grown up on a farm with all that life moving around me, the smells and sounds, the changing seasons, and the life and death a hair's breadth away left a deep imprint on me. . . . I was taught . . . that there was a place in the natural world for all creatures and that creation is bigger than us and we've got to respect that.*
>
> —From Lee's Story

Conscious connection calls us into a transformed relationship based on honesty and integrity. Integrity means complete and undivided—*whole*. As we claim our membership in the earth community and acknowledge reliance on the natural world, we're making a commitment to getting real. Conscious connection with the earth community doesn't require a Smoky-the-Bear hat and shovel. The earth community needs teachers, songwriters, song singers, mechanics, bus drivers, politicians, chimneysweepers, bankers, and virtually every other occupation you can name.

Conscious connection is not about your job; it's about *who you are*—a positive, solution-seeking player in the life we all share. Conscious connection is about living in the largest sense—living connected with self and others, connected with earth, and connected with Spirit. This brings the gift of belonging that you long for, it offers the grounding you need, and the nurturing you have always deserved. The word *human*, like *humus*, means organic soil. We are of the earth. Carrying *conscious connection* is strong medicine—in fact, it's the only medicine.

The dream in your heart invites you make the big commitment: to pledge yourself to becoming free of addictions and distractions, and to be as healthy as possible—one choice at a time, one day at a time, and one meal at a time. This is about paying attention to what you eat, what you do, where you spend your money and your life force, and the awareness you bring into everything about your life. This is no small potato, but it is doable when you break it into smaller bites. You may have heard the saying "Think globally and act locally." That's what we're suggesting. Thinking globally, in this situation, means having an ideal you in mind—knowing how you want to live, not what you do, but the values and commitments you keep. Acting locally means doing the next right thing, guided by those values and commitments, one step at a time. The next chapter contains a process of value clarification to help you identify the qualities that are the most important to you.

No-Honk Zones

Conscious connection begins as we disconnect for a time from the cultural buzz in which we live and experience a slower quieter part of ourselves. In this "no-honk zone," discernment begins. This necessary quality of consciousness begins as you sort through the beliefs and patterns you have lived by to see what is true for you and what consciousness means to you. It is up to you to decide what you keep and what you let go. Free choice is the name of the game—an informed and connected free choice.

Avoid limiting yourself by what you *think* you can do or what you are *supposed* to do. The creative process needs you to let go of your practical side for a while. That means taking *shoulds and oughts* off the table and sorting it out later.

The Power of Acceptance

Making a conscious connection is rooted in the acceptance of what is. We let go of destructive beliefs, feelings, and behavior patterns through acceptance, which is one of the first steps in transformation. Begin the process of acceptance by believing you have always done your best given the circumstances of your life. If you can't believe that now, imagine that you can. Your brain will eventually embrace the idea. It is *already* creating a neural network and receptors to support acceptance. If you say you can't imagine it, ask yourself what it would feel like *if* you could imagine it. Transformation is working below the surface. Have patience and keep on keeping on—you are worth it.

Ask yourself if you are ready to let go of the belief that blocks you. If yes, give it to God, Higher Power, or your Spirit People. Bless it and let it go—respectfully. You can't *make* something go away. You can only allow it to leave. Gratitude opens your heart and allows that to happen. Your job is to get out of the way and avoid actively engaging the belief or behavior. *This is living in faith.* Give yourself time to enjoy the space you've created inside yourself—space for more acceptance. You'll be guided through a process of letting go (getting out of your way) in your medicine bag at the end of this chapter.

Feeling the Feelings of Your Hopes and Dreams

Feelings are our connection; they are our common ground. Feelings connect us to ourselves and with each other. Most addiction and compulsive behavior is about trying to *manage* feelings—ours or someone else's. Before recovery, managing our feelings meant dulling them, disconnecting from them, or heightening them. Despite wanting to manage them, engaging in this behavior disconnected us from our feelings, often leaving us unable to identify what we were feeling. Feeling your feelings is the way back home.

In practicing the exercises at the end of this chapter, feel the feelings of your hopes and dreams fully. When you tap into negative feelings associated with past experiences that block you from your hopes and dreams, acknowledge them by saying to yourself, silently or aloud, "*Yes, I did feel that way at the time. . . .*" Keep it brief, and avoid indulging the negative story. Switch to positive language by saying to yourself, silently or aloud, "*And now I am learning to feel this way. . . .*"

Blocks exist in the brain's limbic system as old emotional memories— but they feel very real. As you feel the block and then consciously choose to feel the hope of your new dream, you are updating and reprogramming your system—you are telling your brain you are *here now* and also letting it know where you want to go. The brain follows your instruction. You want to energize the feelings of your hopes and dreams, while not allowing the old story to get up and running. Repeat the process whenever you find yourself bumping into these old emotions. Take a moment and reconnect with the feeling of your new dream and the story that supports it. Over time, your brain will build the receptors for the new dream and the old one will fade away.

INSIDE THE MEDICINE BAG:
Tools for Awakening Consciousness

The following exercises are highly transformational and can be intense, so be sure to take your time working through them. You will be awakening aspects of yourself that you have possibly been out of touch with for a long time. Read through them before choosing the one you'd like to start with. Skip any that don't speak to you. Remember to work slowly and repeat exercises as needed.

Exercise 1—Exploring Your Hopes and Dreams

Your journey in consciousness begins by exploring your hopes and dreams. This is the first step in claiming your truth. To explore your hopes and dreams, consider these questions:

- What do I long for?
- What does it feel like?
- What about life hooks my imagination?
- What does that feel like?
- What would I do if I weren't afraid?
- What would fearlessness feel like?

Writing down your answers in your journal makes them more powerful. Sharing them with someone else makes them even more powerful. While transformation is personal, it happens best when we work together. Keep your list handy, as you will be referring back to it during these exercises and as you practice them in the future.

Exercise 2—Dreaming the New Dream

Find a quiet place where you won't be interrupted for an hour or so. Get comfortable, relax, and allow yourself to get in touch with your deep hopes and dreams. You might begin with the question we often ask kids, *What do you want to be when you grow up?* If you have any trouble finding an answer, give the question more time. Put it on the back burner. There is no need to rush to find your answers. Your brain is wired for curiosity and creativity—it likes wondering, and it will find your answer. You don't have to know before you know.

Next, change the focus from your career goals to the type of person you want to be. What qualities or characteristics do you want to embody? For example, transformation encourages us to live from the heart, cultivate a positive mind, be of service, and live honestly. What values or characteristics would this require—for example, creativity, bravery, humor, cooperation, peace? In your journal, make a list and don't worry about how you can develop these qualities. They are on the human hard drive; you just have to download them and live them. From the items on your list, pick the top three— the ones you *most* want to have in your life. Now select one, and *imagine* how it *feels* to have this quality.

Experience this quality emotionally, and breathe it in fully. Keep imagining your life with this quality until you can feel it physically. Notice where in your body the feeling resonates. Toxic beliefs that cloud your new vision begin to come to mind, giving you the opportunity to choose to invest in them further or let them go. Some will dissolve on their own. Others may require deeper investigation. This is you transforming into you.

Exercise 3—Transforming Blocks

Taking the top quality you identified in the second part of Exercise 2, close your eyes, and breathe down into your belly. Speaking to *wise mind* (the intuitive part of you), ask what gets in the way of fully living the quality you have chosen to embody—for example, if you chose the quality creativity, ask, "What is blocking me from experiencing my creativity?"

Sit quietly with that question while your deep memory searches the files. *Did someone tell me I wasn't creative (or beautiful or handsome or wonderful . . .)? Did I believe it? Do I need to believe it now?*

There may be more than one message or belief involved, but you don't have to locate every single thing that's part of the block. Often one or two toxic messages will unlock the whole mess. This process is natural; allow it to happen rather than putting demands on yourself.

Exercise 4—Dreaming the Real You

Anything less than loving yourself indicates you are living a nightmare, not dreaming an awakened dream. This exercise will help you get out of the bad dream and into the one that was written on your heart by your creator.

Talk, write, and/or draw pictures about your transformed life and your ideal self until you feel the feelings of it and it begins to feel like it's yours. Notice where in your body you feel these emotions, and breathe into those areas, grounding them in your body—*giving them life.* Practice consciously breathing into the feelings or the sense of your ideal self for several minutes each night as you are going to sleep and again when you first wake up. At those times and at intervals throughout the day, the brain naturally slows down into what are called alpha brainwaves—a highly creative and healing state of mind. During those intervals, energizing your dream is most effective.

As you imagine your ideal self and your transformed life, notice what blocks you from fully entering this new dream. Notice where your mind wants to take you—for example, you might find it saying things like *"Wake up and get real; you're just daydreaming," "Life isn't like that," and "Yeah, right . . ."*

Write these blocks down or create a drawing or other piece of art that represents them. Often, there may be additional subconscious beliefs holding you back, such as *"I don't deserve . . .," I can't do . . .," "I'm just crazy; it's useless . . .," "If I change, it will mean I was wrong all these years . . .,"* and so on.

When you have identified the blocks and are ready to give them up, create a ceremony in which you will symbolize letting them go and allowing them to transform. Fire and water are traditional symbols of transformation. A ceremony can be as simple as burning paper in a fireplace or throwing a rock into a river and watching it sink. Or it can be more elaborate. Add drums, rattles, music, dance, and whatever else comes to mind to your ceremonies if it feels organic to your process. Hold the focus during the ceremony creating clarity of intention and singleness of purpose. Having at least one other person as a witness adds power to the process.

Take time to focus on the feelings and really feel them as you are preparing your ceremony. Questions may come to mind such as, *Who will I be if I let this go? How will others react to me? What will happen to my "old" me?* Our conditioned brain resists change. That's just what it does, but it doesn't need to stop you. Your imagination is more powerful.

When you imagine, you are directing the brain to go where you want to go. (Warning: this is true of worrying, too. We tend to create what we are imagining. You might want to put a leash on imagining bad stuff!) Notice where in your body the feelings of fear resonate. Breathe into them. Then, as you exhale, release them fully from your cells and breathe them out. Now imagine the healed you.

Keep the image of the healed you firmly in your imagination. As you commit your old beliefs to the fire or water, notice how you feel. Take several deep breaths, focusing on the exhalation. The new breath comes automatically, bringing new life. Feel the freedom of letting go and trusting. This is transformation in progress.

Breathe into your chest and place your hand on your heart and feel it beating. You are free of the blocks and ready for a new life. Allow a first step toward your dream to emerge from your heart, moving you toward your authentic desires. It can be a simple action—the important part is that it comes from your heart. Your heart will lead, as you are ready to move more fully toward your ideals.

❖ ❖ ❖

Letting go of beliefs we have carried throughout life can be challenging, but it is totally possible. It's not unusual to repeat and repeat and repeat your efforts—each time reaching deeper into yourself. You are clearing patterns that have come down through your genetics for generations. It's like peeling the onion—one layer uncovers another and another and another. In cases of childhood trauma, the patterns are stored deep in the limbic system, and, in addition to your sincere intention and steadfast attention, healing them may require therapeutic assistance. The limbic system can be updated. You can heal. Don't give up before the miracle, and get more help if you need it.

CHAPTER 24

Setting Your Internal Compass

"If you don't stand for something, you'll fall for anything."

—author unknown

V alues are qualities we appreciate; they create the internal rules by which we make choices. They guide how we run our lives, how we spend time and with whom, where we work, what we do when we aren't working, and how we spend our money. Despite our most sincere attempts to live our values, gaps between what we believe and how we act are not uncommon.

If the gap increases, we may need to change our behavior, and we many need to reassess our value—asking ourselves questions like *Is this a value? How much do I value it? Am I willing to go against my value?* In doing this, we identify our inner conflict; we bring it to conscious awareness. When we don't become aware of conflict, we are experiencing varying degrees of discomfort—from mild to intense—and when we get too uncomfortable, we're going to do something about it. This often results in relapsing back into the substance or behavior we are letting go.

Valuing is an action word—it implies engagement with an ongoing process. Values can change. We might value something at one time in life and find that we don't hold it in such high regard in another time. And there are core values that don't change much over a lifetime. Valuing your life includes reflecting on your values, assessing them, and renewing your commitment to them—making adjustments according to your growing awareness.

Living by values makes life easier, and it also complicates things. Sometimes we have competing values. For instance *freedom* is a value, and *responsibility* is also a value. These two values can seem to be at odds with each other in various situations. When that happens we have to stop and reevaluate our position. We might have to restructure our commitment. This might sound like waffling, but, much to the contrary, it requires deeper involvement and a more mature and responsible relationship with ourselves. Values are not black or white, and very few if any are absolute—they are ideals about which we make conscious choices on our way to authenticity.

Values speak clearly in some situations, and other times we have to sit and listen to our inner voice to find out what is going on inside and determine an appropriate course of action. To add complexity, how we apply our values can change under different circumstances—in those times we encounter the *sit* in *sit*uation! We are in a process of discernment, and perhaps we need to seek advice—sound it out with others. We do that in 12-Step meetings, with a sponsor, in group therapy, or with a trusted friend. Depending on the impact of the decision, wrangling with our values can be intense.

Overall, our value code makes life run smoother by providing principles that assure consistency and integrity. Values aren't laws, but they speak at a deep level. They are written on our heart. Going against them repeatedly creates stress and distress—it can even drive you to drink! This chapter is about clarifying and honoring your values.

"Normal" Is a Cycle on the Washing Machine

Many who have felt excluded from mainstream culture—even those who have gone to great extremes to separate themselves from it—still measure themselves by what is considered *normal* by mainstream culture, or, as we referred to it earlier, the cultural matrix. It's good to remember that *normal* is a cycle on the washing machine. Perhaps *healthy* is a better goal, along with the realization that much of mainstream culture does not reflect good health or balanced living. Regardless, many recovering folks imagine eventually regaining full membership among the "normal" population—or at least they imagine that they will *feel* normal. Again, it's good to recall that the general population isn't feeling all that good! Maybe going for *normal* is aiming too low.

Spirit Recovery and 12-Step recovery—as well as most other spiritualities—are about living in the world shoulder to shoulder with others who may be living by a different code while staying true to yours and not feeling, thinking, or acting as if you are better than they are. Values make this possible. Key recovery values include honesty (to self and other), love and respect for fellow travelers expressed through service, and cultivating a spiritual connection with a Higher Power through prayer and meditation.

From there, everything we have dreamed of doing is possible. The spiritual life is about listening for God's will to be revealed in our day-to-day encounters with life, rather than drawing our lessons from the cultural playbook or withdrawing from life. As the saying reminds us: *being in the world but not of it.* Integrating spiritual life with "real" life allows a lightness of being that smacks of happy, joyous, and free most of the time.

It would be nice if the difference between conforming to the world and being true to our values was obvious, but the lines are regularly blurred. That's where consciousness counts. We have to be present in our body—fed, rested, and aware to get to the signals that let us know we are crossing the line.

> *I had always accepted my emotional reactions as justified. Anger, fear, sadness, joy—I had never considered that I might be more responsible for how I react to my emotions. If I was really going to call myself an adult, I was going to have to be an adult in my relationship with my emotions.*
>
> —From Lee's Story

Values, rather than emotion and reaction, become our internal compass. They point us in the direction of what we hold near and dear—we then have to walk the talk. Principles are the external application of our values—where the rubber hits the road. Identifying our values and being able to define practices that reflect them is an ongoing effort. As a culture, we hold certain values and practices in common. However, culture is not oriented on spiritual principles and is therefore subject to materialism, or you might say subject to the market place. For example, billions of dollars are spent on advertising with the goal of influencing your behavior, specifically how you spend your money with little or no regard for the bigger picture of how this impacts your health or well-being. This doesn't make them bad; they are following the secular cultural rules—playing the game. It's your job to pay attention and make conscious choices.

Living your values is a practice in consciousness, awareness, choices, and responsibility. It's the real deal.

INSIDE THE MEDICINE BAG:
Tools for Awakening Consciousness

The five exercises described in this Medicine Bag can be highly transformational. Read through them before choosing the one you'd like to start with. Skip any that don't speak to you. Remember to work slowly and repeat exercises as needed.

Exercise 1—Core Value List

Below is a list of some of the core values involved in the process of transformation.

- Humility
- Honesty
- Openness
- Loving response in all situations
- Responsibility for your choices
- Attention to health and well-being

Personalize the above list to include your own core values; eliminate any from the list that don't speak to you.

If you belong to a group, have a group discussion on the importance of these values and how to apply them to your life. Practice keeping an open mind while listening to others. If you don't belong to a group, respond in your journal.

Exercise 2—Exploring Values

In the following chart, choose the values that speak to you the loudest. Rate them from 1 to 5 with 5 indicating a high value. Skip any you don't relate to. Narrow the list down to your top ten and write the list in your journal. Next, further narrow the list down to five and, in your journal, rank them according to their importance in your life. You might value something and know you're not very faithful to it but want to be. That's a value—count it—unless it's on your list because you think it *should* be! *Avoid shoulding!* This exercise is between you and you for you. These are your *ideals*. They will become your code of honor. Recognize that you are a work in progress.

VALUES	Low				High
ACHIEVEMENT (accomplishment)	1	2	3	4	5
ACCOUNTABILITY (trustworthiness, being responsible)	1	2	3	4	5
ADVANCEMENT (getting ahead)	1	2	3	4	5
ADVENTURE (new challenges, experiences, healthy risk)	1	2	3	4	5
AESTHETICS (beauty, artistic expression, surroundings)	1	2	3	4	5
AFFECTION (warmth, loving, caring)	1	2	3	4	5
AFFILIATION (participation, involvement, belonging)	1	2	3	4	5
COOPERATION (getting along with others, teamwork)	1	2	3	4	5
DIVERSITY (variety of experiences, appreciating differences)	1	2	3	4	5
FAME (being famous, popular)	1	2	3	4	5
FAMILY (feeling happy, secure, safe)	1	2	3	4	5
FORGIVENESS (pardoning, letting it go—really!)	1	2	3	4	5
FREEDOM (autonomy, choices, self-determination)	1	2	3	4	5
FRIENDSHIP (intimacy, trust, close relationships with others)	1	2	3	4	5
FUN (enjoyment, happiness, humor)	1	2	3	4	5
GRATEFULNESS	1	2	3	4	5
HAPPINESS (contentment, joy, pleasure)	1	2	3	4	5
HEALTH (practicing good self-care)	1	2	3	4	5

VALUES	Low				High
IMAGINATION (creativity, new ideas, seeing things differently)	1	2	3	4	5
INDEPENDENCE (freedom from dependence or control)	1	2	3	4	5
INTEGRITY (consistent with beliefs)	1	2	3	4	5
JOY (lightness of being)	1	2	3	4	5
LOYALTY (devotion, trust, faithfulness)	1	2	3	4	5
ORDER (organization, safety)	1	2	3	4	5
PERSONAL DEVELOPMENT (realizing potential)	1	2	3	4	5
POWER (ability, skills, authority, influence)	1	2	3	4	5
RELIGION (strong beliefs)	1	2	3	4	5
R-E-S-P-E-C-T (valued, status)	1	2	3	4	5
SECURITY (freedom from worry)	1	2	3	4	5
SELF-RESPECT (pride, self-esteem, self-appreciation)	1	2	3	4	5
SERENITY (contentment, inner peace)	1	2	3	4	5
SERVICE (being useful to others, improving society)	1	2	3	4	5
SPIRITUALITY (connected with the sacred)	1	2	3	4	5
WEALTH (making money, getting rich)	1	2	3	4	5
WINNING (excellence, accomplishment, being the top dog)	1	2	3	4	5
WISDOM (understanding life, good sense, fair decision)	1	2	3	4	5

VALUES	Low				High
Add your own:	1	2	3	4	5
Add your own:	1	2	3	4	5
Add your own:	1	2	3	4	5

Exercise 3—Living Your Values

Using the top five values from your list, look at how you are living them. You can have a value and not be currently honoring it and count it, but, if you aren't making headway at all, you might want to reconsider it or make a plan and take steps toward it. In your journal, write down your first value, and answer the following questions:

- How do you honor this value in your life today?
- What are some ways you can further integrate this quality into life?
- Write down your second value, and answer the questions.
- Do the same for each of your top-five values.

Exercise 4—Exploring Human Needs and Rights

In addition to values, we hold certain human needs in common. Needs connect us when they are being met and run the risk of separating us when they aren't being met. Since they are common to the human experience, it is safe to say they are God-given rights. If you are struggling with getting a core need met and questioning the validity of your need, it's helpful to know that your expectations are reasonable. We have a right to feel supported and valued along with other core needs listed in the following exercises. Becoming clear about your rights can give you the footing you need to make healthy changes.

The following is a *partial list* of human needs and rights.

Affection	Kindness
Autonomy	Meaning
Belonging	Peace of mind
Celebration	Physical sustenance
Empathy	Pleasure
Equality	Regeneration
Friendship	Safety
Healing	Self-realization
Honesty	To be known
Joy	(Add yours)

The following is a *partial list* of how we feel when our basic needs are being met:

Affectionate	Included
Confident	Inspired
Creative	Involved
Engaged	Joyful
Excited	Loving
Exhilarated	Peaceful
Grateful	Proud
Hopeful	(Add yours)

The following is a *partial list* of what it feels like when our needs aren't being met:

Angry	Embarrassed
Anxious	Fearful
Ashamed	Hopeless
Confused	Pain
Devalued	Sad
Depressed	Suspicious
Disconnected	Vulnerable
Distrustful	(Add yours)

Exercise 5—Exploring "Power"

Power is a human need and universal value. From where or from whom do you draw your sense of power? To whom or to what do you give your power? In your journal, explore your understanding of power—both acquired and innate. How willing are you to own your innate power? What does that mean to you? What would that require? How would that affect your close relationships? How does your understanding of power affect your recovery? You may want to go back to Chapter 19 and look at the discussion on *power over* and *power within*.

CHAPTER 25

Creating Awareness in Relationships

"Keep people in your life who truly love you, motivate you, encourage you, enhance you, and make you happy. If you know people who do none of these things, let them go."

—From everydaylifelessons.com

Spirituality is about relationship—with ourselves, with others, and with Spirit. Whether we know it or not, we are in relationship with everyone and everything. Recovery is a natural time for considering who and what will accompany you on your journey of transformation.

Aho Mitakuye Oyasin is a Lakota greeting and prayer that means "we are all related." It acknowledges and honors the wholeness of life, which we have been discussing throughout this book. This chapter is designed to help you develop an *awareness* of the human relationships in your life and how they symbolize the relationship you have with yourself, Spirit, and life itself.

The age-old practice of bringing spiritual awareness to our relationships is found in many different cultures. The version shared in this chapter comes from the Q'ero people of the Andes. It is designed to help you create spiritual awareness in your relationships. Understanding the nature of your relationships from a spiritual perspective helps create *right relations*, in which you are not overvaluing or undervaluing yourself or the other person. You have the power of choice. In recovery terms, we're talking about creating non-codependent relationships.

Codependency in Relationships

Codependency describes a system of beliefs, emotions, and behaviors in which one overvalues or undervalues themselves or another in a relationship, which is often the source of enormous pain, making relationships of all types difficult. Codependent relationships are particularly problematic with those with whom we are the closest. The inability to create and sustain healthy relationships is considered by many to be an underlying cause of addiction and other obsessions and compulsions. Whether codependency is the cause of addiction or the effect, the spiritual-based practice in this chapter offers a new understanding of *relationship* itself—relations based in spirit and lived from the heart rather than in anger and fear and with a lot of second-guessing.

The Major Relationships in Your Life

Creating right relations begins by listing all the major relationships in your life. You might organize them according to categories or activities, listing the people who are important to you under those general headings. The list might include groups of people such as your family and neighbors, religious community, school, job, hobbies, sports, and so on, considering everything in your life's wheel to be a relationship.

Sit with your lists and see what aspects might be combined into the same relationship category. For instance, maybe you hike and run and enjoy biking. Depending on how you identify these activities, you might group these as *sports* or *healthy activities* or *exercise*. Under the heading *recovery*, you might include your home group, your therapist or life coach, and your sponsor—listing them individually or as a group. This is about you owning your truth—not what you think you're *supposed* to feel, but what you actually *do* feel.

When you feel like you have the major relationships identified, spend time going back through your list and *feeling* into each relationship. Connect with all the aspects of that relationship—*feel* the connection, breathe with it, and breathe into it. Hold the energy of that relationship in your being, becoming aware of how it feels when you focus on that relationship. This part of the process is about *feeling and awareness of those feelings,* rather than about thoughts or reasoning.

Selecting Symbols to Represent Your Relationships

After connecting emotionally with your relationships and feeling the emotions as they resonate in your body, begin looking for objects to symbolize them. Symbols might be a stone, a coin, a crystal, or a figure—something that represents the important connections in your life based on how you feel about them or the energy they hold in you. These are just examples. Allow your heart and imagination to be your guide. Remember, this is for you. You can't do it wrong. Spend time selecting your symbols, but avoid obsessing over finding the *exact* right symbol. An object you select as a symbol will cooperate with you. It will take on what you ask it to do.

Begin by finding a symbol to represent you. (*Lee's note:* The object I chose to represent myself was a Mexican 10-peso piece. I always liked Mexican money and had a particular connection to that coin, so for many years my symbol in my medicine bag was a shiny 10-peso piece. I also have a couple of small rocks for my work and a tiny plastic baby that represents my daughters. There was also a token from my old 12-Step program that was my recovery practice for many years.)

Once you have gathered the objects that represent your relationships, place them in a square piece of cloth or leather, a scarf, a special bag large enough to hold your tokens, or, if you have one, a Mesa cloth (a handwoven ceremonial bag for carrying objects). This will serve as your Medicine Bag.

Contemplating Your Relationships

Take your tokens and your Medicine Bag to a quiet place where you can sit without distraction. Spread the cloth on the ground and lay the tokens on the bag. Rather than simply looking at the symbols of the relationships, *contemplate* them. Contemplation is more interactive than *looking at*. It allows for a conversation and a new awareness to emerge. Pick up each piece and hold it between your hands as in prayer. Hold the symbol against your heart. Remember, you aren't thinking; you are feeling in your body. Close your eyes and *feel* into the energy of each relationship as it lives in you. Breathe into the space where this relationship exists in you and blow that energy into the token, giving it life.

Imagine a light opening a channel between your heart and the symbol, connecting these living worlds together. By your intent and your breath, you are connecting your heart with the symbol you're holding, forming a living relationship. You are bringing the token to life. When you feel the connection, fully lay that piece down and pick up the next one and repeat the process. Allow time and space between each encounter to listen to your heart and listen to the spirit of that relationship—hear what it is saying to you. Make the connection, then move on to the next one until you have connected them all. Now you are ready to bring them together as a collective embodiment of the relationships that make up your life—the matrix, the system, or pattern that exists inside you.

This is going to take some time, and there is no need to rush—you are awakening your intuition and creating a new consciousness. There is a lot of energy in the network of human relations you have woven in your life. Spend as much time as needed to allow your awareness to develop.

If you are using a cloth, place all the tokens in the center of the cloth and fold it like a present and tie it with a string, ribbon, or strip of leather or cloth. If you are using a pouch, hold each piece and blow your breath into it before placing it inside the bag. Then, tie the bag closed with a string, ribbon, or strip of leather or cloth.

Holding your Medicine Bag in your hands, set your intention—for example, to allow this practice to serve you in coming clear and clean in all your relationships.

Intention gives your permission to the process. This is not to say Spirit doesn't override our intentions when they aren't good for us, but an important aspect of your new consciousness involves *conscious cooperation*. As you become more aware of your old beliefs and patterns, you become more aware of how you project your needs, desires, fears, and expectations on your relations to the extent that you are actually not in relation with anyone but are having a relationship within and with your imagination. No wonder you feel lonely and isolated—and maybe more than a bit confused!

Spending Time with Your Medicine Bag

If it is possible, set aside an hour each day to sit with your Medicine Bag. That may sound like a lot of time, but is it really? This is a connection between you and all the major relationships that make up your life. This is where you spend a good part of your life energy—it's where you express yourself spiritually. It's where you gain insight into your relationship with God. If you can't spend an hour a day, set aside as much time as you can.

In the daily practice, hold your Medicine Bag with love and gratitude for the life you are living. Hold it up to the light of the sun and say a prayer to your God or to your Spirit People to be with you and help you in your Spirit Recovery Journey.

—Lee

Listening with Your Heart

When your heart tells you that you are ready, open the Medicine Bag and spread out the tokens. Look at them carefully and notice which seems to speak to you first or which one you want to speak with first. As you awaken and strengthen this new consciousness, you discover the nuances of working intuitively. You become more certain of what's being said to you by your inner voice. This happens naturally as you set your intention (give permission) and follow your heart. It happens as you pick up each token and breathe deeply with it and blow your life force into the object connecting energy inside you with the object—acknowledging your essential oneness. Ask yourself the questions in the Medicine Bag section at the end of this chapter.

Rewards and Responsibilities of Spiritual Commitment

Your Medicine Bag will take on a life of its own that you'll feel when you pick it up and hold it. As a living thing, relationships are always in the process of change. You will learn to appreciate the good times, increase your ability to endure the uncomfortable times, and learn to make creative decisions as you listen to what your intuition is telling you. You will gain insight and wisdom. Most of all you won't be overly dependent on your relations nor will you be afraid of them.

Spirituality is paradoxical. You'll gain a sense of self that transcends the rules of ordinary relationship—a sense that you are *essentially you* having a relationship with the individuals and groups in your life and *organically one* with them at the same time.

Tokens will come and go as issues or behaviors heal and change. As your intuition develops you'll know when to release a token from your Medicine Bag or when to add one. Be faithful to your practice but not obsessive or rigid. You are not defined by the practice; you are living it by choice and from your integrity or truth. A new practice takes focus, and a new focus takes time. If you forget or find it difficult, give yourself a break and get back to it as best you can. Think in terms of three months to complete this part of the practice and then continue your relationship with the Medicine Bag in a less intense, but deeply meaningful and mindful way.

Spiritual practices are designed to be practical—to build problem-solving spiritual skills that you can draw on in a pinch when you need them. However, relationships require tending. You can't stick your

Medicine Bag away in the closet and expect the relationship to stay vital. Treat your Medicine Bag like a sacred object and handle it like a prayer—with reasonable regularity. You'll notice more happy, joyous, and free time in *all your relations* (*Aho Mitakuye Oyasin*).

Rewards and Responsibilities of Spiritual Relations

The practice of sitting and dreaming into our Medicine Bag creates presence and awareness in our relationships; it invites us to take responsibility for our part in them but not all the responsibility—right relations have give and take. Spirit Recovery practices are done with gratitude and attention to the gift of life. Healing and personal growth come as a result of our willingness to open to possibilities and new points of view. This is a practice of focus, responsibility, attention, and most of all—*love*.

"If I Could Turn Back Time ..."

Life is always shifting and changing. We create problems by holding on to our experiences (usually the painful ones), holding on to judgments we have made or taken on from others (usually the painful ones), and holding on to stories we create about all of that (usually the painful stuff). We repeat these stories in our head and in our conversations with others. We define our self and the world around us by those stories and judgments. Some of the conclusions we have drawn about ourselves and about life are based on the experiences of a very young child. Beliefs often turn into rules, and too many rules—whether they are our own or from others—might keep us out of trouble, but they can also limit our engagement with life, with our willingness to try new things, and with our creativity.

The thinking side of the mind holds beliefs that are based on past experiences and information given to us by others, rather than by our own trial and error. It projects these beliefs into new experiences—overlaying real time. That side of the mind is very determined to be right and clings to what it "knows" as reality. It *insists* on making it seem true. The thinking mind is always a step behind real time because its job is to interpret our experiences, which are in the other hemisphere of the brain. This becomes problematic when the mind has been conditioned with all sorts of critical judgments and preconceived ideas. It will distort our perception of life and limit the possibility of having a new experience to be consistent with what it believes it "knows."

Of course we need beliefs. We need to learn from life or we would keep sticking our hand in the fan. We also need to be consciously aware of our beliefs and be able to hold them lightly, step back a bit while we take a fresh look at something, and make changes in our beliefs when appropriate. The flip side of this happens when we're stuck in the other side of the brain and don't ever draw any conclusions or learn anything from our experiences. We are flying through life by the seat of our pants, sometimes doing the same thing over and over and expecting different results—a popular definition of insanity! We need both sides of the brain to be working together—in relationship with each other to be in successful relations with others and with life.

Beyond the Right/Wrong Matrix

Our thinking mind is vulnerable to being programmed—*conditioned*. It gets invested in knowing and being right. It's no wonder we argue so much defending our opinions. The thinking mind believes it is *supposed* to know. When not knowing equates with being a failure, and failure means unlovable, we will fight to the finish. Consider for a moment how education is organized. You are supposed to know things on your test and fail if you don't know enough answers. And you are supposed to guess when you don't know them. There isn't any box on the test marked *I don't know, but I'd like to!*

The Medicine Bag practice is about resolving the past and getting into real time—new experiences and new interpretations about yourself, your relationships with others, and life itself. It helps you let go of *good and bad* and *right and wrong* as primary filters in your inner system, and it gets you in touch with *intuition and instinct along with consciousness of your updated value code*. Such a transformed system allows you to determine what is appropriate according to circumstances in the moment—informed by the past, but not a prisoner of the past.

We each have our version of reality. We cling to what we know because it gives us a sense of security and identity. We can say, "I know who I am!" "I know who you are!" But we cannot know the internal world of anyone else when we are projecting our version of reality on him or her and on the situation. We can only know a person when we listen to what he or she is saying without running it through our filters. And the reverse is also true. We can't be known when we are hiding behind our filters. The essence of intimacy that we all need and seek happens when the filters are off.

Putting the suggested effort into your relationships may seem time-consuming, but life is lived in relationship. We are not in this game as solo players. The Lakota prayer *Aho Mitakuye Oyasin* doesn't stop with our close family and friends, it extends to *all of creation*. The way we hold our friends and family, our relationship with the animal kingdoms, and the earth itself is a reflection of how we honor our self and how we honor life.

INSIDE THE MEDICINE BAG:
Tools for Awakening Consciousness

Spread out the tokens in your Medicine Bag and choose one for this exercise (you can repeat the exercise with the others). Sit in silence, and hold the token and meditate with the energy of the relationship it contains. Ask yourself the following questions, and listen deep inside to the answers, honoring your intuition.

- How does this relationship feel right now?
- What is the foundation of this relationship? How did it come to be, what is my role, what are my expectations? Am I being completely honest with myself and with the other person in this relationship?
- What do I need to let go of in this relationship and what do I want to keep?
- How can I be of greater service in this relationship and how can this relationship be of greater service to my truth?
- Are there issues here? What are they? Are the issues in me or from the other end of this relationship? Be honest and try shifting your point of view.
- What progress am I going to commit to in this relationship— growth, healing, forgiveness, and acceptance?
- How does this relationship support or jeopardize my recovery and growth?

Ask any other questions that come to mind and be willing to wait for the answers. They come in time—often later when you're hiking the trail or driving on a familiar route or gardening or doing something rote that doesn't require thought. If you rush the process, you'll be driven by angst—meaning you'll be thinking you *should* be somewhere you aren't or that something *should* be happening that isn't. You'll be in the same old space and will just get the same old answers. The new answers arise out of a new consciousness—when they are ready. You can tell the difference between new awareness answers and "same ole same ole" answers.

CHAPTER 26

Following Your
Inner Road Map

*"Our own body is the best health system
we have—if we know how to listen to it."*

—Dr. Christiane Northrup (1950–), author, mind-body medicine pioneer

Throughout the book we've talked about the importance of being in your body where instinct and intuition are felt and where life is lived. And we have talked about Spirit's presence. This chapter now discusses an ancient Hindu teaching and a new field of scientific study to provide insight into how we are guided in life. If you have ever felt like you were operating without a map, you might be relieved to discover that the directions have been included in the package!

Our Instruction Book

Chakra is a Hindu word meaning spinning wheels of light. It refers
to the energy systems that keep us alive and healthy—our life force.
There are seven major chakra centers in the body corresponding to our
major nerve and endocrine centers. They nourish our physical systems
and prompt us in our psychological and spiritual development and
they hold our instincts. Each carries a particular aspect of consciousness and together they can be considered the instruction book for the
human journey. Chakras are awakened at intervals throughout life
and are influenced both positively and negatively by our life situation.
However, our instincts are more powerful than our conditioning and
they will survive intact as we examine our conditioning and choose
what is true for us.

While we experience ourselves in solid form, we are energy vortexes
existing within a larger energy field. Today this field is known as the
quantum field. Quantum science was discovered in the early part of the
last century, significantly changing the laws of physics. Scientists are
still learning more about this amazing phenomenon. We touched on
the quantum field in Chapter 19 and we'll do so again in this chapter.
Keep in mind, though, we are only tapping the surface.

Theologians and holistic healers have their own ideas about the
quantum field's larger meaning. Similar to many indigenous people,
they understand this field as an intelligent spiritual force—continuous
creation unfolding. Some have gone so far as to say it is Creator's presence, here and now. Invisible to see with the naked eye, the quantum
field is made of subatomic particles moving at lightning fast speed.
These particles, called quanta, seem to be the substance out of which
everything is formed and within which everything exists. We are
calling this apparently unlimited source *the breath of life, the soul of
creation*. This breath of life breathes us.

Personal consciousness is the degree to which we are aware of and in communication with this sacredness. As our awareness grows we move beyond thinking of God or Great Spirit as a separate being and we begin experiencing *the essence of being—our wholeness.*

Human Journey Fail-Safe

According to ancient Hindu teachings, our life map is imprinted in energy centers in the body. In addition to providing health and well-being, these centers can troubleshoot. Things go wrong in life— sometimes seriously wrong. People that are supposed to love us hurt us and we hurt others whom we love—and we hurt ourselves. Many times these injuries are traumatic. As a result our thinking gets distorted, negative feelings such as shame and self-hate can overwhelm us. Over time health is compromised. We may turn to addiction or other compulsive behaviors as medication to distract us from our pain—but that eventually makes things worse. Fearing that we are so bad or so badly injured that we are beyond repair, we lose hope.

Spiritual lessons teach us that our soul is whole and complete. Our belief that we are doomed is illusion and the feeling of brokenness can heal. Awareness of our potential to transform can make the difference when we choose to believe.

Seven Sacred Gates: The Chakra System

The chakras function as unified whole. They are numbered from bottom to top but value isn't implied by the ascending order. All of the centers contribute to our development. The first three create our foundation. They activate in infancy and throughout childhood and into our teens. During these formative years, we are dependent on caretakers and family to help us ground our spirit into physical life. As we learned in Chapter 20, family dysfunction is common. Many of us get off to a rough start. The fourth chakra helps us heal the past and sets us on the path to discovering our true self. The top three chakras provide the means of living our spiritual truth. There are other energy centers throughout the body. We're focusing on the seven major ones.

I realized that the power in healing the wounds and beliefs that under-mined our truth would allow each of us to live the "happy, joyous, and free" that life offers. Recovery is really about the power of personal responsibility and the grace of courage of compassion in action.

—From Lee's Story

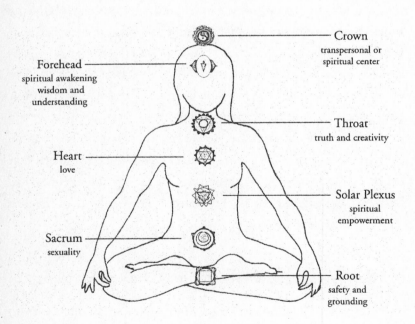

Forehead —
spiritual awakening
wisdom and
understanding

Heart —
love

Sacrum —
sexuality

Crown
transpersonal or
spiritual center

Throat
truth and creativity

Solar Plexus
spiritual
empowerment

Root
safety and
grounding

Chakra System in Human Body
The chakra system is numbered from
1st to 7th from bottom to top.

1. Root Chakra

The root chakra is located in the lower spine, called the sacrum. It's our base. Root chakra holds the basic pattern for physical, emotional, and spiritual healing. It energizes our spine and the central nervous system. It's essential for health and well-being. Root chakra awakens in infancy, bonding us with our caretakers. We are dependent on them for survival and for establishing patterns of safety and security.

As we mature, this chakra contains the primal pattern for making a family and raising the next generation. For those who aren't pursuing family life, it energizes self-care, caring for others, and vocations that express the values listed below. Root chakra grounds our life force as a human being energizing all human endeavors. All healing begins in energizing the root chakra.

- Root chakra is represented by the color red.
- Values: self-care, health, home, family, community, nature, peace, nurturing, security, and hope.
- Physically: it affects the large intestine and the rectum and influences the function of the kidneys.
- Consciousness: root chakra's awareness is undifferentiated— meaning in early life we don't distinguish ourself from family in our perception or our experiences during the first years of life. Whatever is happening in the family imprints on the child. We are *one* with the tribe, absorbing the attitudes, beliefs, and behaviors of this primary group—learning from them.

When the energy in root chakra is strong and flowing we feel safe and secure. It provides the foundation for healthy development setting us up for life. When safety and security are not established in infancy and early childhood, our life force is weakened, our health is threatened, and we will struggle with issues of betrayal and trust—trusting the wrong people, trusting too much, or an inability to trust at all—until it is healed.

Root Chakra Affirmations

"I am safe; I belong."

"I am healing and I ask for help."

"I am where I am supposed to be in my healing journey and in my life."

"My life is unfolding and I'm not finished yet."

"I have the right to be me."

Create your own affirmations, focusing on the feelings of belonging and safety. Remember you don't have to believe what you're saying; you are creating a new belief system. State affirmations as if they have already happened; I am, rather than I will be. However, when it comes to safety, you can't override your instinct with affirmations. If you are not safe, you have to make corrections to assure your safety—seek guidance.

See Appendix II for more information on healing chakras and how they relate to 12-Step recovery.

2. The Sacral Chakra

The sacral chakra is located in the belly behind the bellybutton. It's our emotion center and where intuition and instinct are felt. It holds the energy for creativity, procreation, sex (sexual energy is located in both the first and second chakras), and self-control. Empathy begins here and develops as we are treated with respect and fairness at a young age. This chakra contains the energetic seeds for individuality as our perception of self awakens and we begin seeing ourselves as an individuate within the family—although we won't actually be an individual until the teen and young adult years. Sacral chakra holds the energetic instinct for relations with others as healthy relationship depends on a healthy sense of self.

- Sacral chakra is represented by the color orange.
- Values: empathy, fairness, friendship, equality, self-worth, sexual choice, emotional freedom, relationship, partnership, and choice.
- Physically: it energizes the organs of the lower belly, the reproduction system, the testicles, and ovaries, and the bladder and kidneys.
- Consciousness: sacral chakra contains our emotional sensitivity, creativity, empathy, intuition, and idealism. It corresponds to a child about two years of age up to eight or nine, the years of magical thinking. Healthy development in this part of life becomes the source of happy, joyous, and free. This marks the beginning of good decision-making, happy relationship, and a creative engagement with life.

Trauma interrupts healthy emotional development and codependency can begin. We might avoid relationships altogether or be obsessively involved in them, losing self in the process. We might be overly sexual while avoiding commitment or intimacy. We might lack the independence to see ourselves as decision-makers. Emotional development is compromised, and our connection to intuition is weakened. Our natural sense of creativity is challenged.

Sacral Chakra Affirmations

"I am a perfect child."

"I am learning to love myself."

"My emotions are real but they aren't always facts."
"I release negative feelings and I am free."
"I am creative and I follow my dreams."

Add your own affirmations, using images that reflect self-appreciation and creativity.

3. Solar Plexus Chakra

The solar plexus chakra is located above the waist and below the heart. It generates self-esteem and willpower. It contains our potential to engage life—to be us, to make choices and take responsibility for them. Personal power is necessary for establishing boundaries, and for feeling strong and comfortable in the world. Boundaries contain us and they keep others from invading our space. This chakra takes us across the bridge from childhood to becoming an adult. Rights of passage such as bar and bat mitzvahs and the sacrament of confirmation are important markers for a maturing young person, allowing them to see themselves as powerful. This passage is a tipping point. Paradoxically, this is when we often get seriously off course and it is also the source of the energy of transformation.

- Solar plexus is represented by golden yellow.
- Values: personal power, the ability to make things happen, free will, independence, integrity, loyalty, justice, responsibility, choice, freedom, adventure, and discovery.
- Physically: it energizes the digestive system, liver, gall bladder, stomach, spleen, autonomic nervous system, pancreas, and the small intestine.
- Consciousness: solar plexus chakra contains the directions for right use of power, expressing ourselves through free will and

accepting the consequences of our choices. It feeds healthy
ego and activates our further movement into the adult world.

When this energy is flowing, we feel confident. We know who we
are and can act independently, while staying true to our ideals. This
chakra corresponds to teen years. Rather than rebellion, it is a time
of high idealism—confronting hypocrisy in healthy ways. Loyalty
shifts from family to peer group as we further individuate. Personal
power and free will along with responsibility are all necessary qualities for adulthood.

Trauma can result in self-will running riot, rebellion, or paralyz-
ing inaction—limiting our ability to be effective in the world. When
healthy independence is not encouraged, when our emerging self is
not given room and guided respectfully, self-confidence suffers. Feeling
powerless can be expressed destructively in grandiosity, manipulating
or being easily manipulated by others. Our natural ability to put our
ideas into action lags. Addiction often begins in this period, and we
stall out on our journey to adulthood.

Solar Plexus Chakra Affirmations

"I am powerful and I take responsibility for how I use my power."
"I make good decisions."
"I am confident, courageous, and aware."
"I am a positive force in the world."
"I have the power to make things happen."

*Add your own affirmations, focusing on empowerment, strengthening
your will, your ability to make good decisions, and taking responsibility.*

4. Heart Chakra

The heart chakra is located slightly left of center in the chest. Interestingly, the Sanskrit word for this chakra is *Anahata,* meaning "un-struck." It is the gateway to higher self. We must heal the issues of childhood and adolescence to participate fully in life and in our journey. Our awakened heart loves us completely. It heals without judgment and translates to our ability to fully love others. It's where our Inner Healer resides.

- Heart chakra is represented by the color green.
- Values: love, empathy, understanding, compassion, wisdom, generosity, justice, honesty, forgiveness, courage, beauty, contribution, peace, and spirituality.
- Physically it energizes the heart, midback, upper ribcage, chest, skin, circulatory system, lower lungs, abdominal cavity, and thymus gland.
- Consciousness: heart chakra awakens our ability to experience self-love and love beyond self-serving needs. Heart consciousness carries forgiveness of self and others, trust, compassion, and peace. It nurtures generosity of spirit, empathy, brotherly and sisterly love, romantic love, and humanitarian love.

When my first daughter was born, I learned what true love felt like. I had experienced feelings that I thought were love, but they weren't. Holding that little girl touched a part of me that remembered the truth of life. She was my baby, and my love for her was unconditional.

—From Lee's Story

When heart energy is flowing we meet challenges effectively and are able to recover from losses and disappointments that come our way. We understand human frailty with compassion and are able to love others as they are. We have mastered self-forgiveness and forgiveness of others.

Childhood injuries can leave us confused, feeling stuck in resentments and bitterness and ultimately shame, and isolation. We are caught in the struggle of life, living at survival level, feeling heavy and joyless. Yet the heart is always open. Guilt, both appropriate to our actions and guilt that rightfully belongs to others keeps us from experiencing the love we crave. Heart is a guilt-free zone!

Heart Chakra Affirmations

"I choose love."

"I surrender shame, blame, and the beat-me-up game."

"Love flows to me and through me."

"My heart gives me courage as I heal."

"I am forgiven."

Add your own affirmations, focusing on the power of love to heal.

5. Throat Chakra

Throat chakra is located behind the collarbone. It energizes clear communication—speaking our truth and listening to others with our heart. It provides the energetic push to seek our truth and to express it. Like the second chakra it activates creativity—communicating our authentic self through art, music, writing, and living creatively.

- Throat chakra is represented by the color blue.
- Values: truth, clear communication, honesty, creativity, authenticity, free speech, free thought, and humor.

- Physically: it relates to the nervous system, eyes, ears, nose, throat, lungs, vocal cords, bronchial system, throat, jaw, neck, nape of neck, and thyroid and parathyroid glands.
- Consciousness: throat chakra energizes our hunger for truth. It seeks freedom and encourages us to live fearlessly. It embodies open-mindedness and attunes our ear to hear the deeper meanings in others' words. It also guides us to be silent when appropriate.

When throat energy is flowing it indicates that we have resolved earlier trauma and conflict. We are in our truth, living authentically and creatively. Our communication with self and others is open and sensitive.

If throat chakra has been jeopardized by childhood trauma, we have trouble finding our voice. We hedge and dodge the truth, trying to keep safe. Honesty is compromised at all levels—making it hard to know who we are and live our truth. Creativity is stifled. This indicates that further time with the heart is needed.

Throat Chakra Affirmations

" I am a work in process."
"My words have power."
"I speak from my heart."
"I empower others by careful listening."
"My actions reflect my truth."

Add your own affirmations, considering the gifts of this chakra—the power of truth, insight, and clear communication.

6. Third Eye Chakra

This chakra is located in the center of the forehead. It holds the pattern for integration, bringing insight, depth, and understanding to our life journey. It indicates a high degree of consciousness—right thinking and right action. Spiritual awakening, comprehensive vision, and wisdom are associated with third eye.

- Third eye chakra is represented by the color violet.
- Values: global vision, wisdom, beauty, justice, compassion, spirituality, peace, truth, service, living by principles, valuing life, and appreciating the journey.
- Physically it energizes the eyes, nose, ears, brain, pituitary gland (main hormone balancer), and white blood cells.
- Consciousness: third eye chakra corresponds to the prefrontal cortex, the seat of ethics and moral choices. It energizes purpose and vision. It connects us to our priestly or shamanic role of servant in the world.

When this energy is flowing we are in *wise mind*. We have embodied our values and are living a spiritually integrated life. We have worked our way though life's dilemmas and are able to be fully present to others. We hold a higher-order vision for humankind's search for peace, love, justice, and mercy.

If trauma has not been healed, we might misuse our spiritual power. Rather than carrying a message of love and mercy, we might "preach" condemnation. We might make false assumptions about who or what higher power is and impose our view on others.

Third Eye Affirmations

"I am grateful."

"I surrender."

"I appreciate life."

"I choose to live with purpose and vision."

"I give thanks."

Add your own affirmations, considering the gifts of this chakra—gratitude, clear vision, and service.

7. Crown Chakra

The crown chakra is located just above the top of the head, connecting us energetically with the cosmos and beyond. It is sometimes referred to as "the crown of God." It signifies fulfillment of our spirit. It is the seat of higher consciousness and the portal to eternal life. It's believed that our spirit leaves our body through crown chakra at the time of death.

- Crown chakra is represented by the color purple.
- Values: love, empathy, compassion, and completion.
- Physically: it energizes the endocrine or pineal glands and white blood cells.
- Consciousness: has moved beyond judging; we embrace the human condition as it is and others as they are. In doing that we create a *zone of liberation* in which people feel profound acceptance and are thus assisted on their journey. Crown chakra embodies awareness of unification. Spiritual truths are understood from all perspectives. It is the source of great joy.

The energy in this chakra reflects a high degree of awakening or what is also called enlightenment. It carries awareness of life beyond this world but does not act "other worldly." It is grounded in the reality of this life.

The Crown Chakra Affirmations

"I surrender to the beauty and mystery of life."

"I respect right use of spiritual powerful."

"I receive guidance of divine source."

"I allow light to flow through me, bringing light into the world."

Add your own affirmations that celebrate the consciousness of the crown chakra as you connect with the fullness of life.

INSIDE THE MEDICINE BAG:
Tools for Awakening Consciousness

The following practices are helpful for balancing your chakras and becoming more familiar with your inner road map. Reminder: How the chakra system corresponds to 12-Step recovery along with specific instructions for healing can be found in Appendix II on page 268.

1. Crown chakra is like chakra "headquarters," it holds awareness of the whole system. Spiritual practice involves meditation and affirmations for all seven centers, energizing and balancing the whole system. Consider using the crown chakra meditation as part of your regular practice.

   • Begin by sending your attention down through the root chakra into the earth until you feel grounded. Express gratitude for the miracle of life.

   • Bring your attention into your belly feeling it rise with the inhalation and soften as you exhale. Express gratitude for the company of fellow travelers.

   • Bring attention into the solar plexus and breathe deeply. Express your gratitude for free will and your willingness to take responsibility for your life.

   • Bring attention into your chest and breathe deeply. Place your hand over your heart and feel the love that is there. Express gratitude for life. Allow this energy to expand into the world.

   • Bring attention into your throat and feel breath coming into your nose and down your throat. Express gratitude for living in truth.

   • Bring attention to your forehead and breathe deeply. Express gratitude for being of service in the world.

- Bring attention to your crown charka and feel your connection to the cosmos. Breathe deeply and express gratitude for being a clear vessel for others.

2. Draw an image of the chakra system and color it. Spend time contemplating each of your energy centers. Write a new story that reflects your hopes and dreams as if they are already accomplished. Refer back to the qualities associated with each chakra and weave them into your story. In writing this new story, don't hold back—make it as ideal as possible. Notice the feelings that accompany your new story.

3. Then go for it! Take one step toward letting your new story come true.

Conclusion

We hope we have encouraged you to do your dance, sing your song, and live the life that's in you! We believe life works best when we're connected to our body—and moving toward our dream. In doing that, you will encounter the naysayers, the unbelievers, and those who are just plain jealous that you have the spunk to go for what's in your heart. Bless them and keep moving forward. We believe that life can be happy, joyous, and free most of the time. When it isn't, there is a way to look at our situation and our relationship to it differently and get back to happy, joyous, and free—not by settling, but by accepting the new lesson and adjusting your belief system accordingly. This involves awareness, intention, conscious effort, reflection, and resetting your compass in an ongoing practice. It's you being open to the flow of life.

Our insistence throughout the book on getting grounded in nature and connected to your spirit is foundational to a successful human journey—all the rest hinges on that. If you disconnected or shut down somewhere along the way, you did it for a good reason. You protected yourself until you got to a time and place where you could reconnect or, in plain talk, get back on the horse and ride! Nature has provided the means to heal us, but we have to be in our body to partake of her medicine.

Now get along and do your dance and sing your song and send us an occasional postcard along the way.

For more information on Spirit Recovery,
visit www.spiritrecovery.com
or write to the authors at
Integrative Life Center
1104 16th Avenue South
Nashville, TN 37221
1-877-334-6958

APPENDIX I

The Breath of Life

Meeting Your Inner Healer

We are self healing. That is not to say we don't need help in the process, but healing is part of the human experience. Wounds heal, bones knit back together, and we recover from great losses. And at the same time, some diseases and injuries are beyond our ability to heal in the way we imagine healing. However, with assistance, support, and time we can change our relationship with our illness or injury. Our experience of trauma, no matter how bad, can heal. We can transcend our circumstances. Transcendence is more likely to happen when we are in peaceful mind—not when we are in survival mode. Let's see how this works.

Meet Your Inner Healer

The central nervous system is composed of the brain and spinal cord. It is central to the human experience; virtually responsible for maintaining life and consciousness at all levels—it is our awareness of life. Out of the vast and complex network of nerves, fibers, and functions that make up the brain and spinal cord, we're going to focus on two particular functions of the autonomic nervous system—a system within the system that is key to maintaining balance and order in our inner world. It is a two-phase process: the sympathetic cycle and the parasympathetic cycle. We're calling this dynamic duo the *Inner Healer*.

These two aspects of a whole operate together in a cooperative relationship. The sympathetic nervous system takes care of our life systems, monitoring heart rate, respiration, blood pressure, and other basic life support systems. It's our action side of the cycle. It also governs our flight or fight stress response, activating it when it's important to get out of the tiger's path. Its partner, the parasympathetic cycle is often summarized as our rest and digest system. It operates as our being side of the cycle in a complimentary way to the more action driven sympathetic side. It relaxes us and allows us to normalize after times of stress. We can engage it through deep breathing, pulling our energy into us, and limiting our contact with the external environment until we settle down. These functions relate to brain waves, which are described in the next section. When everything is going reasonably well in our lives the autonomic nervous system takes care of business effectively without us even being aware of it. We feel like we're in the flow of life and that is exactly where we are.

Experiencing stress on an ongoing basis, when it becomes our way of life, the partnership within this life support system breaks down. We get stuck in the sympathetic function and this creates an anxiety cycle. We are flooded with stress chemicals. And the more stress we experience the more chemicals get pumped into our bloodstream and the more stressful we become. Anxiety builds and the parasympathetic cycle, now overwhelmed with stressful chemicals will most likely not activate on its own. This can be described as being caught in a trauma response.

Without some kind of intervention, it's unlikely that we'll be able to reestablish the necessary equilibrium to maintain health and well-being. This can become a breakdown moment or a breakthrough one. Although when you are in the middle of it, it's hard to tell the difference. This is where consciousness comes into the picture. When you are aware of your inner workings and can activate a healthy response, you have the opportunity to intervene and change the pattern.

Severe trauma, both past (post traumatic stress syndrome) and currant trauma upset our natural order—throwing us off balance. Another part of the brain activates and the game changes; it takes over the system. It believes we are in danger whether in real time or in memory. It disables our ability to discern past from present and memory from event. Severe trauma generally needs professional intervention.

The very first therapeutic intervention in a trauma response is connection. This happens first through the breath. Following the pattern that nature installed in our system—deep breathing, pulling our focus into the body and limiting contact with the outside world, we can interrupt the run-a-way sympathetic response and restart the parasympathetic cycle. Further therapy involves introspection, identifying triggers that threw you off course, learning to breathe through them, changing the internal dialogue and making changes in your behavior. We've taken you through some of these processes in the book and, as stated earlier, if you are not experiencing the relief you need, seek the further help of a professional.

Traumatic Brain Waves and Healing Response

Trauma, including prolonged stress, scrambles the brains normal wave patterns. Brain waves are measured in hertz (Hz) or cycles per second. There are four main brain wave states: beta, alpha, theta, and delta, each with their own consciousness. And a fifth one called gamma but science has not come to an agreement about it and it isn't always included in brain wave discussions. The trauma response is largely occurring in beta wave state, in energy spikes described below. The relaxation response (first called that by Dr. Herbert Benson) occurs in alpha brain wave state. The downshift from beta to alpha is spontaneous (thank you, Inner Healer) when things are running smoothly. We can also influence this shift by our breath—the six to ten deep intentional breaths you've been reading about.

Beta brain waves (14 to 40 Hz) reflect a cognitive thinking and logic consciousness. Beta is mostly how we relate in the external world—outside self. It's our doing brain wave. It corresponds to normal waking consciousness, when we are using critical thinking skills, analyzing and interpreting, sorting, and storing information. Healthy beta measures in the 14 to 21 Hz range. It "spikes" into much higher range—40 to 60 Hz when we are alerted to pay attention to potential danger. Generally when the event is over we calm down. However, in traumatic situations and when we have chronic anxiety, we stay in dangerously high numbers for long periods of time stressing our entire system. The trauma response, as described earlier, occurs in prolonged beta with dangerously high spiking.

Alpha brain waves (7 to 14 Hz) reflect a consciousness of imagination, creativity, and restoration. It's when we make ourselves new again. Alpha corresponds to the relaxation cycle described earlier. Alpha waves are also considered the gateway to the unconscious and to deeper slower waves. You must pass through alpha brain waves to get to sleep. They're our daydreaming cycle corresponding to our night dream cycle. You can induce an alpha brain wave through deep breathing, meditation, and through restful activities such as art, listening to music, taking a walk, sitting in nature. Intuition, insight, and imagination are heightened. Feel good chemicals have been released by the brain and you come away feeling restored.

Theta brain waves (4 to 7.5 Hz) reflect a consciousness of mystery. Its slower beat indicates deep meditation and deep sleep. This is the realm of the subconscious. It can foster a feeling of spiritual connection and that sense of *oneness with all that is* that we have talked about throughout the book. Patterns that exist in the subconscious can be accessed, and profound insight is not unusual during theta waves. Theta enhances creativity and is fertile ground for inner work. Setting your intentions before sleep, giving them to the Inner Healer or saying your prayers, allows sleep to become transformational.

Delta brain waves (0.5 to 4 Hz) bring a consciousness of connection and deep healing. Delta waves are the slowest frequency. They are experienced in deep sleep and in very deep meditation. In the lower levels of delta they indicate unconsciousness—a comalike state. This is a place of profound healing. You might say alpha relaxations during the day provide necessary tune-ups, and delta offers profound healing. However, for that to occur we have to get a good night's sleep. Metaphysical interpretation describes this brain wave state as the gateway to universal mind.

Gamma brain waves (above 40 Hz) bring a consciousness of integration and profound insight. They represent a slightly different pattern than the other waves—moving back and forth from back to front, it is as if they are binding all the experiences together with the result of achieving a high level of consciousness. While the scientific community is not in agreement regarding gamma waves—what they are and what they measure—these waves have been associated with gifted musicians, artists, those with extraordinary intelligence, and those with outstanding athletic ability. Also, in the brain waves of longtime meditators.

Returning to our topic of breath and healing, we have the most influence in effecting the shifts in consciousness by taking those all-important six to ten deep breaths and chilling out. Adding a meditation practice to your recovery will help in many ways, including improving awareness of needing a breath and time out.

The 20-Minute Cat Nap

We have a built-in system for releasing stress and maintaining health throughout the day. It's called our ultradian rhythm. Ultradian means a personal rhythm as compared to circadian rhythms that tend to affect us all about the same way. According to psychologist Ernest Rossi, our brain waves automatically switch from beta to alpha approximately every 90 to 120 minutes and relieve accumulated stress. These periods last from 10 to 30 minutes. In which time our systems are refreshed. We then switch back to beta, which is our normal healthy brain wave for interacting in the world. We know this as the whisperings of the Inner Healer!

In those ultradian moments it becomes difficult to focus, we feel "spacey." We might find ourselves staring out the window or even nodding off. To reap the most benefits from our ultradian rhythm, we could stretch out on the couch or lean back in a comfortable chair and close our eyes and rest. We can, however, override nature's attempts to keep us healthy and happy, and many of us do. We grab a double latte, or a can of soda, or a chocolate bar or in some other way wake ourselves up.

If we did follow this natural urge, in about 20 minutes we would come back into an awakened state with virtually all systems and organs renewed, clear minded and emotionally centered. Creativity would be enhanced and we would approach problems with a fresh attitude. At the end of the day, we would have handled stress incrementally and we would be ready for a nice evening with family or friends, or alone time with a good book. We would go to sleep shortly after going to bed, and we would enjoy a good night's sleep.

While we can't always take full advantage of these brief interludes—or cat naps—we can understand what is going on and take a small break in routine if only to pull away from the work for a few minutes, lean back, and enjoy a few deep breaths. We could take a walk outside or just go outside for a breath of air. Much of what we're talking about is common sense. However, we have gotten off our internal clock and onto the time clock, perhaps to an unhealthy level. We make choices. Any concession to our natural process will help reduce stress. Eventually we might heed our Inner Healer's advice and take the 20-minute chill out.

APPENDIX II

Healing the Chakra System and 12-Step Recovery

"The physician treats, but nature heals."

—Hippocrates (460–370 BCE), Greek physician

Despite a troubled infancy and childhood, you can heal. Regardless of the addictions, obsessions, compulsions, and whatever else you've done to buffer the pain and keep on keeping on, you can heal.

Read through the following material and begin with suggestions that seem right for you. If nothing seems right or if you don't experience the healing that you need, you may need more support. It takes time for your brain to grow the new neural system that will embody your new consciousness. In the meantime consider getting help from a counselor or spiritual advisor. You can heal, and you don't have to do it alone.

The Root Chakra and 12-Step Recovery

In 12-Step recovery, the first chakra relates to the 1st Step of Alcoholics Anonymous: "We admitted we were powerless over alcohol (or other addictions and compulsions)—that our lives had become unmanageable." The root chakra relates to the need to belong to a safe community—to come in from the cold. We are encouraged to join the fellowship and find a home group. We can have the guidance of a sponsor, who often fills in the role of enlightened spiritual parent, offering support and encouragement as we come to terms with our unmanageable life. Good sponsorship and the fellowship activate our root chakra energy system, which generates the healing process.

1. Tips for Healing the Root Chakra

Like each of the Steps in 12-Step recovery, all of the chakras are equally important. Whenever you are struggling in your recovery 12-Step wisdom says, go back to the beginning—Steps 1, 2, and 3. They correspond to chakras 1, 2, and 3.

- Sit on the ground with your legs crossed. Your spine, buttocks, and upper thighs form a triangular base, making a solid connection with the ground. Begin with conscious breathing, pulling the breath up from the earth into your feet, legs, and lower spine, and then exhaling completely. As you inhale

imagine you are pulling strong vital energy up into your body.
As you exhale imagine that you are releasing toxic thoughts or
feelings. Continue this exercise until you feel a sense of relief.
Spending time with this meditation creates a sense of safety in
which healing happens.

- Maintain an orderly environment. Chaos creates confusion
  and confusion is stressful. Order creates safety and allows
  peace of mind. If you are overstructured, try correcting toward
  more spontaneity, but too much spontaneity creates instability.
  In that case you might need more structure. Aim for the
  middle ground.

- Organize your time—reset your body clock with regular
  mealtimes and bedtimes. Use an appointment calendar and
  practice getting to your appointments on time—this probably
  involves leaving on time. Avoid rigidity. Leave space open in
  your schedule for spontaneity. While scheduling spontaneity
  may seem like a conflict in terms, if we don't schedule free
  time, we don't seem to ever get around to it.

- Make sure you are safe in your home. If you are not safe
  get help from a counselor familiar with family-of-origin
  dynamics. Safety comes first.

- Create a meditation space using elements from the earth.
  Rocks, pinecones, moss, flowers, or plants, for example,
  are helpful reminders of your connection to the "Mother
  Ship" and ultimately to your body. Hold one of these earthy
  elements as you spend quiet time simply breathing, securing
  your place on the earth.

Sacral Chakra and 12-Step Recovery

In 12-Step recovery, the consciousness of this chakra is expressed in the 2nd Step "Came to believe that a power greater than ourselves could restore us to sanity." In recovery, we are reconnecting to our emotions—awakening repressed ones and learning how to manage overwhelming ones. Mood swings make us feel crazy! We recognize the emotional turmoil of addiction and the confusion of growing up in an addictive household, and we are healing from childhood wounds. We are discovering choice and how we can choose a new path. We explore our relationship with our higher power and with one another, listening to one another's stories and learning how we are alike and how we are different. Friendships we form in early recovery are vital to our growth and development as a person as well as to our successful recovery.

2. Tips for Healing the Sacral Chakra

Healing this chakra begins by breathing down into your belly, feeling it rise and fall with each breath and noticing the emotions that are awakened. Notice them and let them move through you without judging them or judging you. Consider writing them down in a journal or notebook. You can find lists of basic emotions online that are helpful in developing emotional language and gaining emotional awareness. Negative self talk interferes with healing.

- Surrender self-blame, self-judgment, self-criticism, and any other negative patterns you are holding whether you can name them or not.
- Ask yourself the following questions and write your answers in your journal:
  ◊ How was love expressed in my family? What beliefs did that create in me?
  ◊ How was anger expressed in my family? What beliefs did that create in me?
  ◊ What were family beliefs regarding money—acquiring it and spending it? What beliefs did that create in me?
  ◊ Was I encouraged in my creativity? What beliefs did that create in me?
  ◊ How were my likes and dislikes respected by my family? What beliefs did that create in me?

Finish this exercise by identifying new beliefs you would like to embody. Write your new story based in your truth and share it with someone telling it as if it already happen (saying I am rather than I will be).

- Awareness of our creativity begins in this chakra. Visit an art gallery. Consider taking an art class or explore artistic expression on your own—paint, draw, or simply color with crayons. Listen to music and dance around the room—it stirs up your energy and gets the creativity flowing.
- Meditation for the sacral chakra might include spending time by water. Our body is mostly water and water has a calming effect. You can sit outside by water. Or if that isn't possible, hold a shell or a bowl of water, breathing deeply and allowing

your mind to relax. Soaking in the tub, taking a relaxing shower, sitting by the water, and even holding your hands under running water alerts the subconscious mind to begin the healing process.

The Solar Plexus Chakra and 12-Step Recovery

The third chakra relates to Step 3, "Made a decision to turn our wills and our lives over to the care of God as we understand him." Key elements in the 3rd Step are the words: *decision, will,* and as we *understand him.* These concepts don't imply blind obedience but support a growing need to take responsibility for one's choices and actions. The insistence of the 12 Steps in respecting all ideas about a higher power helps restore personal power. The only suggestion is to imagine your higher power as a loving one. Whether we approach this Step with a diminished will or an imposing one, we are in bondage and are asking to be healed—to be freed. It's important to note that, while many recovering people are healing a boastful ego, just as many are coming from the other side—a diminished one. Both conditions are the result of a wounded sense of self.

3. Tips for Healing the Solar Plexus Chakra

Healing the solar plexus chakra begins by rethinking power. When we deny our power, it comes out in unhealthy behaviors. It would be better to recognize the spiritual origins of all power and learn how to use it wisely.

- The solar plexus chakra corresponds to the teen years and is often when addiction is activated. Addiction stops our emotional maturity from progressing and interferes with making a successful transition from adolescent to adult. It's never too late! Choose someone of your gender at least ten years older who has the qualities you want to develop. In 12-Step recovery, this is often a sponsor. For others it might be a teacher, clergy, a church member, a relative, or a therapist.
- Struggling with issues of power is common—what it is, how to get it, how to use it, and even if you want it. Healthy personal power is natural and necessary. List ways you have sought power noting the results of your attempts. What would it be like to claim your natural organic power and experience it as a spiritual right?
- Hold a fire ceremony. Write down things you would like to see happen in the world—how you would make it a better place. Burn the paper and watch as it is transformed into smoke and ashes. Like the Phoenix your hopes will rise out of the ashes.
- Create a rite-of-passage ceremony claiming your true identity. Choose a descriptive name that reflects your truth. This can be your spiritual name that you may want to keep private—how you use it is up to you. Write your code of ethics. Identify characteristics and values that you want to live by. Write them down and share them with at least one other person.

The Heart Chakra and 12-Step Recovery

Heart chakra corresponds to the process beginning with the 4th Step "Made a searching and fearless moral inventory of ourselves," Mystical Heart becomes Warrior Heart, energized by the courage to face our inner demons and make right the wreckage of the past. During the process, we forgive ourselves and others whom have caused us harm. This is a tall order during which peace and order are restored to our lives. While it is common to approach the 4th Step with fear and shame, Warrior Heart converts fear and trepidation to acceptance and love.

4. Tips for Healing the Heart Chakra

Healing the heart chakra is about self-forgiveness and learning how to love—beginning with loving yourself. All too often we are carrying the guilt that belongs to those who mistreated us. The heart wonders what you would feel like if you chose to spend more time imagining being loved rather than how bad you are. Guilt and shame are demons blocking us from experiencing love. Heart carries the courage to face our pain and heal and to love and be loved. Turn it over to your Inner Healer.

- Imagine a loving relationship with yourself, rejecting all judgmental ideas you levy against yourself.
- If you are on the fence about a higher power, imagine a healing loving presence *beyond* definition.
- Heart chakra encourages balancing your *love-in* and *love-out*

ratio. Determine if you are giving more than you have been getting or holding back and refusing to engage.

- Ask for help discerning what is rightfully your guilt and what rightfully belongs to someone else. Forgive yourself and notice how you naturally begin to forgive others.
- Mediate on what it would feel like to let go of the past and be in love with yourself.
- Put more fun in your life.

The Throat Chakra and 12-Step Recovery

In 12-Step recovery, this chakra is about radical honesty. It relates to the 5th through 10th Step:

Step 5. "Admitted to God, to ourselves, and to another human being the exact nature of our wrongs." It continues through the next five steps as we realize our truth, speak it, and commit to truthfulness—and that we do it with loving spirit.

Step 6. "We're entirely ready to have God remove all these defects of character."

Step 7. "Humbly asked Him to remove our shortcomings."

Step 8. "Made a list of all persons we had harmed, and became willing to make amends to them all."

Step 9. "Made direct amends to such people wherever possible, except when to do so would injure them or others."

Step 10. "Continued to take personal inventory and when we were wrong promptly admitted it."

These six steps in the full context of the 12 Steps provide a pathway to authenticity—living who we are, including our rough edges. They set you up to live a life of service, free of the past, and rooted in your values.

5. Tips for Healing the Throat Chakra

Healing the throat chakra begins with a commitment to get real—to tell our truth. Your creativity is rooted in your truth. Consider ways of expressing yourself creatively.

- Commit to telling the truth in your journal if you don't already do it.
- Try your hand at writing a song, a poem, or even a short story about truth.
- Read the book *The Four Agreements* by don Miguel Ruiz, specifically focusing on the first agreement: be impeccable with your word.
- Practice conscious breathing exercises, taking deep full breathes and exhaling fully. You can do this when you are stuck in traffic, while waiting for the light to change, during TV commercials, or while listening to your favorite music. It helps you keep your cool while reprogramming your breathing at the same time.
- Sing—sing in the shower, sing in your car, sing in the choir and every place you can.

The Third Eye Chakra and 12-Step Recovery

In 12-Step recovery the 6th chakra relates to Step 11, "Sought through prayer and meditation to improve our conscious contact with God, as we understood Him, praying only for knowledge of His will for us and the power to carry that out." It calls us to prayer and meditation and living a spirit-centered life that transcends job or social position, recognizing that all occupations are spiritual vocations when infused with the consciousness of service to fellow travelers. Social rank has no meaning spiritually.

6. Tips for Healing the Third Eye Chakra

This chakra represents a high degree of awareness, but, if it is not grounded in the lower chakras, it can result in rigid thinking, spiritual confusion, or a lack of inner vision. If we are disconnected from our base in the first three chakras, we lose sight of the human condition. This can result in self-righteousness or a holier-than-thou attitude. While we often think of spiritual development as rising above the human experience, the opposite is true. It is rooted in the human experience and doesn't forget its roots.

- Grounding in nature balances this chakra—it keeps us real.
- Volunteering at shelters and organizations that serve others is another good reality check for the third eye chakra.
- Consider forming a prayer circle with friends and pray and meditate on peace and justice for the world.
- Consider sitting with a skilled meditation teacher.

The Crown Chakra and 12-Step Recovery

In recovery, the crown chakra relates to Step 12: "Having had a spiritual awakening as the result of these Steps, we tried to carry this message to alcoholics, and to practice these principles in all our affairs." The crown chakra implies a high degree of spiritual awareness and service. The principle of attraction rather than promotion is actualized in this chakra. Relations to others are characterized by compassion and love. The fully awakened person moves humbly in the world, operating from awakened heart, carrying the message by presence and actions more than words.

7. Tips for Healing the Crown Chakra

Regardless of our level of development, we remain vulnerable to human fragility and can lose perspective. An ungrounded crown chakra can result in spiritual crises—loss of faith or despair. Most well developed people continue being a student. We never outgrow our need for good counsel.

- Contemplate the principle attraction, not promotion, and practice it.
- Contemplate the principle progress not perfection.
- Read the biographies or watch films of people you respect.
- Remember to ask questions.

About the Authors

Lee McCormick has been a creative force in the mental health and recovery arena for more than fifteen years. He is the founder of the Ranch Recovery Center in Nunnelly, TN; and the Canyon Treatment Center in Malibu, CA. He is also cofounder of Nashville's Integrative Life Center and IOP/PHP Community Recovery program in Nashville, TN.

Through the organization Spirit Recovery Inc., McCormick facilitates the production of healing and recovery conferences and spiritual journeys around the world. He is the executive producer of the documentary *Dreaming Heaven*, in which he plays a leading role. This documentary chronicles the experiences of eighteen individuals on a five-day journey at Teotihuacán. McCormick has led many journeys to this place of power and has developed a far-reaching relationship with the mystery of the shamanic world that is present there.

He is the author of *The Spirit Recovery Meditation Journal: Meditations for Reclaiming Your Authenticity* and coauthor of *Dreaming Heaven: The Beginning Is Near!*

McCormick has four daughters and two granddaughters and lives between his ranch in Pinewood, Tennessee; his home in Malibu, California; and the Dreaming House in Teotihuacán, Mexico, with his equally strong-hearted wife, Mee Tracy McCormick (acclaimed author of *My Kitchen Cure)*, and their daughters, Lola and Isabella.

Mary Faulkner holds a master's degree in religious education with a focus in pastoral counseling. Continuing her education, she spent seven years studying with Lakota, Celtic, and Yoruba teachers. She has published eight books exploring religion, spirituality, and recovery. Mary is the former director of women's treatment at Cumberland Heights in Nashville and currently the trauma specialist at the Ranch in Nunnelly, TN. She is the cofounder of the Integrative Life Center in Nashville where she certifies professionals in Integrative Hypnotherapy for Transforming Trauma.

Faulkner is a pioneer in the field of mind-body therapy, creating holistic programming for twenty-five years. She is currently involved in developing curriculum for a program designed to help therapists and counselors bridge the gap between traditional treatment modalities and holistic healing.

Mary enjoys writing, traveling, making flower essences, and spending time with family and friends. She lives on the bank of the South Harpeth River on the western edge of Nashville.

Other Books by Lee McCormick

Dreaming Heaven: The Beginning Is Near! (with coauthors Gini Gentry, Francis Rico, and Kelly Sullivan Walden). Culver City, Calif.: Agape Media International, LLC, 2013.

The Spirit Recovery Meditation Journal: Meditations for Reclaiming Your Authenticity. Deerfield Beach, Fla.: HCI Books, 2006.

Other Books by Mary Faulkner

Women's Spirituality: Power and Grace. Charlottesville, Va.: Hampton Roads Publishing Co., Inc., 2011.

Easy Does It Meditation Book and Recovery Flash Cards. Charlottesville, Va.: Hampton Roads Publishing Co., Inc., 2008.

Easy Does It Relationship Guide for Recovering Couples. Center City, Minn.: Hazelden, 2007.

Robert Thomas O'Gorman and Mary Faulkner. *The Complete Idiot's Guide to Understanding Catholicism*, 3rd Edition. New York: Alpha [Penguin], 2006.

Easy Does It Dating Guide for People in Recovery. Center City, Minn.: Hazelden, 2004.

Supreme Authority: Understanding Power in the Catholic Church. New York: Alpha [Penguin], 2003.